MW00879839

Illinois State Parks

This Journal Belongs to:

....

....

Packing List

- ☐ CAMERA
- ☐ PARK MAP
- ☐ TRASH BAG
- ☐ WARM SWEATER
- ☐ BINOCULARS
- ☐ MAGNIFYING GLASS
- ☐ WATER BOTTLE
- ☐ SNACKS
- ☐ SWIMSUIT AND TOWEL
- ☐ FIRST AID KIT AND SNAKE BITE KIT
- ☐ HAT
- ☐ SUNBLOCK
- ☐ PEN AND PENCIL
- ☐ BACKPACK
- ☐ FIELD GUIDE
- ☐ DON'T FORGET TO PACK THIS BOOK!

Anything Else?

List of Illinois State Parks

PARK NAME	COUNTY OR COUNTIES	VISITED	DATE
Adeline Jay Geo-Karis Illinois Beach State Park	Lake		
Anderson Lake State Fish & Wildlife Area	Fulton		
Apple River Canyon State Park	Jo Daviess		
Argyle Lake State Park	McDonough		
Baldwin Lake State Fish & Wildlife Area	Randolph		
Banner Marsh State Fish and Wildlife Area	Fulton		
Bartlett Woods Nature Preserve	Lee		
Beall Woods State Park	Wabash		
Beaver Dam State Park	Macoupin		
Big River State Forest	Henderson		
Bohm Woods Nature Preserve	Madison		
Buffalo Rock State Park & Effigy Tumuli	LaSalle		
Cache River State Natural Area	Johnson		
Cape Bend State Fish and Wildlife Area	Alexander		
Carlyle Lake State Fish and Wildlife Area	Fayette		
Castle Rock State Park	Ogle		
Cave-in-Rock State Park	Hardin		
Chain O'Lakes State Park	McHenry		
Channahon State Park	Will		
Clinton Lake State Recreation Area	DeWitt		
Coffeen Lake State Fish and Wildlife Area	Montgomery		
Crawford County State Fish and Wildlife Area	Crawford		
Delabar State Park	Henderson		
Des Plaines Fish and Wildlife Area	Will		
Dixon Springs State Park	Pope		
Donnelley/Depue State Park	Putnam		

PARK NAME	COUNTY OR COUNTIES	VISITED	DATE
Eagle Creek State Recreation Area	Shelby		
Edward R. Madigan State Fish and Wildlife Area	Logan		
Eldon Hazlet State Recreation Area	Clinton		
Ferne Clyffe State Park	Johnson		
Fort Massac State Park	Massac		
Fox Ridge State Park	Coles		
Frank Holten State Recreation Area	St. Clair		
Franklin Creek State Natural Area	Lee		
Fults Hill Prairie State Natural Area	Monroe		
Gebhard Woods State Park	Grundy		
Giant City State Park	Jackson, Union		
Golconda Marina State Recreation Area	Pope		
Goose Lake Prairie State Natural Area	Grundy		
Green River State Wildlife Area	Lee		
Hamilton County State Fish and Wildlife Area	Hamilton		
Harry "Babe" Woodyard State Natural Area	Vermilion		
Heidecke Lake State Fish & Wildlife Area	Grundy		
Henderson County Conservation Area	Henderson		
Hennepin Canal Parkway State Park	Bureau, Lee, Whiteside, Rock Island, Henry		
Hidden Springs State Forest	Shelby		
Horseshoe Lake State Fish & Wildlife Area	Alexander		
Horseshoe Lake State Park	Madison		
Illini State Park	LaSalle		
Illinois Caverns State Natural Area	Monroe		
Iroquois County State Wildlife Area	Iroquois		
James "Pate" Philip State Park	DuPage, Kane		
Jim Edgar Panther Creek State Fish and Wildlife Area	Cass		
Johnson-Sauk Trail State Park	Henry		
Jubilee College State Park	Peoria		

PARK NAME	COUNTY OR COUNTIES	VISITED	DATE
Kankakee River State Park	Kankakee, Will		
Kaskaskia River State Fish & Wildlife Area	St.Clair, Monroe, Randolph		
Kickapoo State Recreation Area	Vermilion		
Kinkaid Lake State Fish and Wildlife Area	Jackson		
Lake Le-Aqua-Na State Park	Stephenson		
Lake Murphysboro State Park	Jackson		
LaSalle Lake State Fish & Wildlife Area	LaSalle		
Lincoln Trail Homestead State Memorial	Macon		
Lincoln Trail State Park	Clark		
Lowden State Park	Ogle		
Mackinaw River State Fish and Wildlife Area	Tazewell		
Marshall State Fish & Wildlife Area	Marshall		
Matthiessen State Park	LaSalle		
Mautino State Fish and Wildlife Area	Bureau		
Mazonia/Braidwood State Fish and Wildlife Area	Grundy		
Mermet Lake State Fish and Wildlife Area	Massac		
Middle Fork State Fish and Wildlife Area	Vermilion		
Mississippi Palisades State Park	Carroll		
Mississippi River State Fish and Wildlife Area	Jersey, Calhoun		
Moraine Hills State Park	McHenry		
Moraine View State Recreation Area	McLean		
Morrison-Rockwood State Park	Whiteside		
Nauvoo State Park	Hancock		
Newton Lake State Fish and Wildlife Area	Jasper		
North Point Marina	Lake		
Pekin Lake State Fish and Wildlife Area	Tazewell		
Pere Marquette State Park	Jersey		
Piney Creek Ravine State Natural Area	Jackson, Randolph		
Powerton Lake State Fish and Wildlife Area	Tazewell		

PARK NAME	COUNTY OR COUNTIES	VISITED	DATE
Prophetstown State Recreation Area	Whiteside		
Pyramid State Recreation Area	Perry		
Ramsey Lake State Recreation Area	Fayette		
Randolph County State Recreation Area	Randolph		
Ray Norbut State Fish and Wildlife Area	Pike		
Red Hills State Park	Lawrence		
Rend Lake State Fish and Wildlife Area	Franklin, Jefferson		
Rice Lake State Fish and Wildlife Area	Fulton		
Rock Cut State Park	Winnebago		
Rock Island Trail State Park	Stark, Peoria		
Saline County State Fish and Wildlife Area	Saline		
Sam Dale Lake State Fish and Wildlife Area	Wayne		
Sam Parr State Fish and Wildlife Area	Jasper		
Sand Ridge State Forest	Mason		
Sanganois State Fish and Wildlife Area	Cass, Schuyler, Mason		
Sangchris Lake State Recreation Area	Christian, Sangamon		
Shabbona Lake State Park	DeKalb		
Shelbyville State Fish and Wildlife Area	Moultrie		
Sielbeck Forest Natural Area	Johnson		
Siloam Springs State Park	Adams, Brown		
Silver Springs State Fish & Wildlife Area	Kendall		
Snakeden Hollow State Fish and Wildlife Area	Knox		
Spitler Woods State Natural Area	Macon		
Spring Lake Fish and Wildlife Area	Tazewell		
Starved Rock State Park	LaSalle		
Stephen A. Forbes State Recreation Area	Marion		
Ten Mile Creek State Fish & Wildlife Area	Hamilton, Jefferson		
Trail of Tears State Forest	Union		
Tunnel Hill State Trail	Johnson, Pulaski, Saline, Williamson		

PARK NAME	COUNTY OR COUNTIES	VISITED	DATE
Turkey Bluffs State Fish and Wildlife Area	Randolph		
Union County State Fish and Wildlife Area	Union		
Volo Bog State Natural Area	Lake		
Walnut Point State Park	Douglas		
Washington County State Recreation Area	Washington		
Wayne Fitzgerrell State Recreation Area	Franklin, Jefferson		
Weinberg-King State Park	Schuyler		
Weldon Springs State Recreation Area	DeWitt		
White Pines Forest State Park	Ogle		
William G. Stratton State Park	Grundy		
William W. Powers State Recreation Area	Cook		
Wolf Creek State Park	Shelby		
Woodford State Fish and Wildlife Area	Woodford		

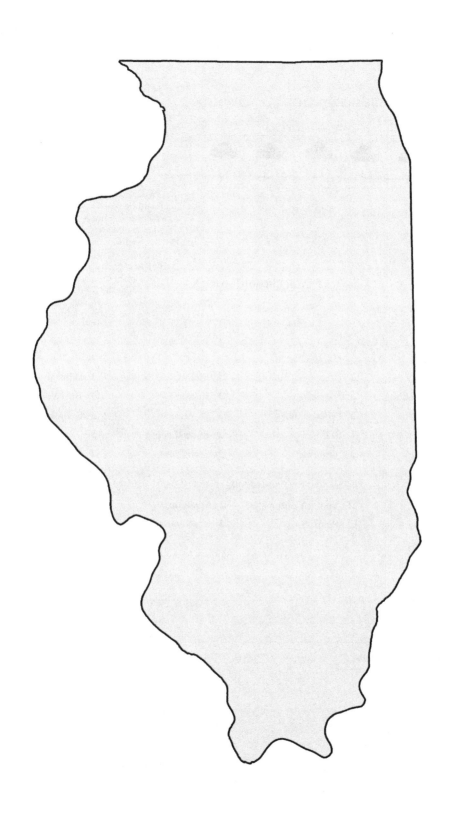

ADELINE JAY GEO-KARIS ILLINOIS BEACH STATE PARK

Lake

DATE(S) VISITED:..

❑ SPRING   ❑ SUMMER   ❑ FALL   ❑ WINTER

WEATHER	TEMP:
☀ ❄☁ ☁ 🌧 ⛈ 🌦	
❑ ❑ ❑ ❑ ❑ ❑	

Check In:................................ Check Out:................................

Lodging:.................................. Park hours:........................

Who I Went With:...

Fee(s):.. Will I Return? YES / NO

Rating ⭐ ⭐ ⭐ ⭐ ⭐

ABOUT THIS STATE PARK

The park is broken into two units that encompass an area of 4,160 acres and contains over six miles of Lake Michigan shoreline. Recreational activities at the park include boating, swimming, hiking, bicycling, camping, bird watching, and picnicking. Known primarily for the beach, the park also includes dune areas, wetlands, prairie, and black oak savanna. The area at the far southern end of the park is a designated nature preserve, which was named a National Natural Landmark in 1980.

Activities

❑ ATV/OHV	❑ Horseback Riding	❑ Fishing	❑ Wildlife
❑ Berry Picking	❑ Kayaking	❑ Hiking	❑ Bird Viewing
❑ Biking	❑ Photography	❑ Hunting	❑ Snowmobiling
❑ Boating	❑ Skiing	❑ Snowshoeing	❑ ....
❑ Canoeing	❑ Skijoring	❑ Swimming	❑ ....

Facilities

❑ ADA	❑ Visitor Center	❑ Museum	❑ ....
❑ Gift Shop	❑ Picnic Sites	❑ Restrooms	❑ ....

Notes

....
....
....
....

Passport Stamps

ANDERSON LAKE STATE FISH & WILDLIFE AREA

Fulton

DATE(S) VISITED:...

☐ SPRING   ☐ SUMMER   ☐ FALL   ☐ WINTER

WEATHER	TEMP:

☐ ☐ ☐ ☐ ☐ ☐

ABOUT THIS STATE PARK

Anderson Lake is a floodplain lake that frequently receives overflow waters from the Illinois River. The lake has 1,134 surface acres with a maximum depth of 6 feet and an average depth of 4 feet. Carlson Lake is a waterfowl management area of 230 surface acres, with a maximum depth of five feet and an average depth of 3 feet. This area is drained in early summer, planted to feed duck and flooded in the fall to attract waterfowl to the area.

Check In:.............................. Check Out:..............................

Lodging:.................................. Park hours:........................

Who I Went With:..

Fee(s):... Will I Return?   YES / NO

Rating
★ ★ ★ ★ ★

Activities

☐ ATV/OHV
☐ Berry Picking
☐ Biking
☐ Boating
☐ Canoeing

☐ Horseback Riding
☐ Kayaking
☐ Photography
☐ Skiing
☐ Skijoring

☐ Fishing
☐ Hiking
☐ Hunting
☐ Snowshoeing
☐ Swimming

☐ Wildlife
☐ Bird Viewing
☐ Snowmobiling
☐ ....
☐ ....

Facilities

☐ ADA
☐ Gift Shop

☐ Visitor Center
☐ Picnic Sites

☐ Museum
☐ Restrooms

☐ ....
☐ ....

Notes

....
....
....
....

Passport Stamps

APPLE RIVER CANYON STATE PARK

Jo Daviess

DATE(S) VISITED:..

❑ SPRING   ❑ SUMMER   ❑ FALL   ❑ WINTER

WEATHER	TEMP:
☀ ❄ ☁ ☁ 🌧 ☁🌨 ☁🌨	
❑ ❑ ❑ ❑ ❑ ❑	

Check In:.............................. Check Out:...............................

Lodging:...................................... Park hours:........................

Who I Went With:..

Fee(s):... Will I Return?   YES / NO

Rating
★ ★ ★ ★ ★

ABOUT THIS STATE PARK

Apple River Canyon State Park is in the hilly northwest corner of Illinois in Jo Daviess County near the Wisconsin border. Limestone bluffs, deep ravines, springs, streams and wildlife characterize this area. Once a part of a vast sea bottom that stretched from the Alleghenies to the Rockies, the scenic canyon area was formed by the action of the winding waters of the Apple River.

Activities

❑ ATV/OHV	❑ Horseback Riding	❑ Fishing	❑ Wildlife
❑ Berry Picking	❑ Kayaking	❑ Hiking	❑ Bird Viewing
❑ Biking	❑ Photography	❑ Hunting	❑ Snowmobiling
❑ Boating	❑ Skiing	❑ Snowshoeing	❑ ....
❑ Canoeing	❑ Skijoring	❑ Swimming	❑ ....

Facilities

❑ ADA	❑ Visitor Center	❑ Museum	❑ ....
❑ Gift Shop	❑ Picnic Sites	❑ Restrooms	❑ ....

Notes

....

....

....

....

Passport Stamps

ARGYLE LAKE STATE PARK   McDonough

DATE(S) VISITED:..

❏ SPRING   ❏ SUMMER   ❏ FALL   ❏ WINTER

ABOUT THIS STATE PARK

Known as a fisherman's delight, Argyle Lake State Park has a full complement of recreational opportunities. Just 7 miles from Macomb, Argyle Lake also offers picnicking, camping, hiking and boating facilities in a scenic, natural setting. With its 93-acre lake for boating and fishing, 5 miles of rugged foot trails through luxuriant virgin forests and full-service campgrounds, this heavily wooded, 1,700-acre site is the ideal place to spend a day, a weekend or longer.

| WEATHER | | | TEMP: | |

❏   ❏   ❏   ❏   ❏   ❏

Check In:............................. Check Out:...............................

Lodging:................................. Park hours:.......................

Who I Went With:...

Fee(s):... Will I Return?   YES / NO

Rating ★ ★ ★ ★ ★

Activities

❏ ATV/OHV   ❏ Horseback Riding   ❏ Fishing   ❏ Wildlife
❏ Berry Picking   ❏ Kayaking   ❏ Hiking   ❏ Bird Viewing
❏ Biking   ❏ Photography   ❏ Hunting   ❏ Snowmobiling
❏ Boating   ❏ Skiing   ❏ Snowshoeing   ❏ ....
❏ Canoeing   ❏ Skijoring   ❏ Swimming   ❏ ....

Facilities

❏ ADA   ❏ Visitor Center   ❏ Museum   ❏ ....
❏ Gift Shop   ❏ Picnic Sites   ❏ Restrooms   ❏ ....

Notes
....
....
....
....

Passport Stamps

BANNER MARSH STATE FISH AND WILDLIFE AREA

Fulton

DATE(S) VISITED:...

❏ SPRING   ❏ SUMMER   ❏ FALL   ❏ WINTER

ABOUT THIS STATE PARK

Banner Marsh State Fish and Wildlife Area is located approximately 25 miles southwest of Peoria on U.S. Route 24 and is protected from the Illinois River by a major levee. Teeming with fish and wildlife, Banner Marsh provides outdoor activities including hunting, fishing, boating, dog training, picnicking, wildlife observation and photography. Three public access areas lead into Banner Marsh, all of which have parking lots, boat ramps, restrooms and picnic areas.

WEATHER			TEMP:		
❏	❏	❏	❏	❏	❏

Check In:.............................. Check Out:................................

Lodging:.................................... Park hours:.........................

Who I Went With:...

Fee(s):.. Will I Return?   YES / NO

Rating ★ ★ ★ ★ ★

Activities

❏ ATV/OHV   ❏ Horseback Riding   ❏ Fishing   ❏ Wildlife

❏ Berry Picking   ❏ Kayaking   ❏ Hiking   ❏ Bird Viewing

❏ Biking   ❏ Photography   ❏ Hunting   ❏ Snowmobiling

❏ Boating   ❏ Skiing   ❏ Snowshoeing   ❏ ....

❏ Canoeing   ❏ Skijoring   ❏ Swimming   ❏ ....

Facilities

❏ ADA   ❏ Visitor Center   ❏ Museum   ❏ ....

❏ Gift Shop   ❏ Picnic Sites   ❏ Restrooms   ❏ ....

Notes

....
....
....
....

Passport Stamps

BEALL WOODS STATE PARK
Wabash

DATE(S) VISITED:...

❑ SPRING   ❑ SUMMER   ❑ FALL   ❑ WINTER

WEATHER	TEMP:
☀ ❄☁ ☁ ☁▥ ☁ ☁	
❑ ❑ ❑ ❑ ❑ ❑	

Check In:.............................. Check Out:..............................

Lodging:.................................... Park hours:.......................

Who I Went With:..

Fee(s):.. Will I Return?   YES / NO

Rating ★ ★ ★ ★ ★

ABOUT THIS STATE PARK

Located on the banks of the Wabash River in southeastern Illinois, Beall Woods State Park attracts visitors from around the world who are interested in experiencing one of the few remaining tracts of virgin timber east of the Mississippi River. At Beall Woods, visitors can see trees 120 feet tall and more than 3 feet in diameter. Besides hiking, Beall Woods also offers visitors a quiet, relaxing setting for camping, picnicking and fishing.

Activities

❑ ATV/OHV	❑ Horseback Riding	❑ Fishing	❑ Wildlife
❑ Berry Picking	❑ Kayaking	❑ Hiking	❑ Bird Viewing
❑ Biking	❑ Photography	❑ Hunting	❑ Snowmobiling
❑ Boating	❑ Skiing	❑ Snowshoeing	❑ ....
❑ Canoeing	❑ Skijoring	❑ Swimming	❑ ....

Facilities

❑ ADA	❑ Visitor Center	❑ Museum	❑ ....
❑ Gift Shop	❑ Picnic Sites	❑ Restrooms	❑ ....

Notes
....
....
....
....

Passport Stamps

BEAVER DAM STATE PARK

Macoupin

DATE(S) VISITED:..

❑ SPRING   ❑ SUMMER   ❑ FALL   ❑ WINTER

WEATHER			TEMP:		
☀	⛅	☁	🌧	⛈	🌦
❑	❑	❑	❑	❑	❑

Check In:................................. Check Out:...............................

Lodging:.................................. Park hours:........................

Who I Went With:...

Fee(s):.. Will I Return?   YES / NO

Rating ⭐ ⭐ ⭐ ⭐ ⭐

ABOUT THIS STATE PARK

Located in Macoupin County 7 miles southwest of Carlinville and situated in an oak/hickory woodland, Beaver Dam State Park offers a variety of recreational opportunities on its 750 acres. Fishing, picnicking, hiking, and tent and trailer camping are among the most popular activities. Although beaver are virtually gone from this area, the park is named for a beaver dam that created its lake.

Activities

❑ ATV/OHV	❑ Horseback Riding	❑ Fishing	❑ Wildlife
❑ Berry Picking	❑ Kayaking	❑ Hiking	❑ Bird Viewing
❑ Biking	❑ Photography	❑ Hunting	❑ Snowmobiling
❑ Boating	❑ Skiing	❑ Snowshoeing	❑ ....
❑ Canoeing	❑ Skijoring	❑ Swimming	❑ ....

Facilities

❑ ADA	❑ Visitor Center	❑ Museum	❑ ....
❑ Gift Shop	❑ Picnic Sites	❑ Restrooms	❑ ....

Notes

....
....
....
....

Passport Stamps

BIG RIVER STATE FOREST

Henderson

DATE(S) VISITED:...

☐ SPRING   ☐ SUMMER   ☐ FALL   ☐ WINTER

ABOUT THIS STATE PARK

Big River State Forest is a remnant of a vast prairie woodland border area that once covered much of Illinois. Among its vegetation are two endangered plants - penstemon, commonly known as bearded tongue, and Patterson's bindweed, which N.H. Patterson documented in 1873, for the first time anywhere, in the forest.

WEATHER						TEMP:
☐	☐	☐	☐	☐	☐	

Check In:.............................. Check Out:..............................

Lodging:................................... Park hours:.......................

Who I Went With:..

Fee(s):... Will I Return?   YES / NO

Rating ⭐ ⭐ ⭐ ⭐ ⭐

Activities

☐ ATV/OHV   ☐ Horseback Riding   ☐ Fishing   ☐ Wildlife
☐ Berry Picking   ☐ Kayaking   ☐ Hiking   ☐ Bird Viewing
☐ Biking   ☐ Photography   ☐ Hunting   ☐ Snowmobiling
☐ Boating   ☐ Skiing   ☐ Snowshoeing   ☐ ....
☐ Canoeing   ☐ Skijoring   ☐ Swimming   ☐ ....

Facilities

☐ ADA   ☐ Visitor Center   ☐ Museum   ☐ ....
☐ Gift Shop   ☐ Picnic Sites   ☐ Restrooms   ☐ ....

Notes

....
....
....
....

Passport Stamps

BOHM WOODS NATURE PRESERVE

Henderson

DATE(S) VISITED:..

❑ SPRING   ❑ SUMMER   ❑ FALL   ❑ WINTER

ABOUT THIS STATE PARK

The Nature preserve is located northwest of the Southern Illinois University Edwardsville campus, and on the west side of Poag Road. The entrance is at the junction of Poag Road and Bohm School Road. The hunting area consists of 90 acres. The majority of the parcel is composed of upland woodland with several small grassland parcels interspersed on the east and west sides of the property.

WEATHER	TEMP:
☀ ❑ 🌤 ❑ ☁ ❑ 🌧 ❑ 🌨 ❑ 🌫 ❑	

Check In:............................ Check Out:...............................

Lodging:.................................... Park hours:.......................

Who I Went With:...

Fee(s):.. Will I Return?   YES / NO

Rating ★ ★ ★ ★ ★

Activities

- ❑ ATV/OHV
- ❑ Berry Picking
- ❑ Biking
- ❑ Boating
- ❑ Canoeing
- ❑ Horseback Riding
- ❑ Kayaking
- ❑ Photography
- ❑ Skiing
- ❑ Skijoring
- ❑ Fishing
- ❑ Hiking
- ❑ Hunting
- ❑ Snowshoeing
- ❑ Swimming
- ❑ Wildlife
- ❑ Bird Viewing
- ❑ Snowmobiling
- ❑ ....
- ❑ ....

Facilities

- ❑ ADA
- ❑ Gift Shop
- ❑ Visitor Center
- ❑ Picnic Sites
- ❑ Museum
- ❑ Restrooms
- ❑ ....
- ❑ ....

Notes

....

....

....

....

Passport Stamps

BUFFALO ROCK STATE PARK & EFFIGY TUMULI

LaSalle

DATE(S) VISITED:..

❏ SPRING ❏ SUMMER ❏ FALL ❏ WINTER

WEATHER	TEMP:
☀ ❏ ❄☁ ❏ ☁ ❏ 🌧 ❏ 🌧 ❏ 🌨 ❏	

Check In:................................ Check Out:...............................

Lodging:.................................. Park hours:..............................

Who I Went With:...

Fee(s):.. Will I Return? YES / NO

Rating ⭐⭐⭐⭐⭐

ABOUT THIS STATE PARK

Located approximately 3 miles west of Ottawa in LaSalle County, this 298-acre park has long been a favorite picnic area, as well as a nature lovers' delight. The area of Buffalo Rock was the home of the Illinois Indians when Louis Jolliet, the French explorer, and the Jesuit missionary priest Father Jacques Marquette made their trip up the Illinois River in 1673. Later, the Illinois tribe was virtually annihilated in protracted warfare with the aggressive Iroquois.

Activities

❏ ATV/OHV   ❏ Horseback Riding   ❏ Fishing   ❏ Wildlife
❏ Berry Picking   ❏ Kayaking   ❏ Hiking   ❏ Bird Viewing
❏ Biking   ❏ Photography   ❏ Hunting   ❏ Snowmobiling
❏ Boating   ❏ Skiing   ❏ Snowshoeing   ❏ ....
❏ Canoeing   ❏ Skijoring   ❏ Swimming   ❏ ....

Facilities

❏ ADA   ❏ Visitor Center   ❏ Museum   ❏ ....
❏ Gift Shop   ❏ Picnic Sites   ❏ Restrooms   ❏ ....

Notes

....
....
....
....

Passport Stamps

CACHE RIVER STATE NATURAL AREA   Johnson

DATE(S) VISITED:..

❑ SPRING   ❑ SUMMER   ❑ FALL   ❑ WINTER

WEATHER		TEMP:			
☀	❄	☁	🌧	⛈	🌨
❑	❑	❑	❑	❑	❑

ABOUT THIS STATE PARK

Totaling 14,960 acres in Johnson, Massac and Pulaski counties, Cache River State Natural Area is composed of three distinct management units - Little Black Slough, Lower Cache River Swamps and Glass Hill. They provide food, cover and water for an incredible diversity of plant and animal species, more than 100 of which have been listed as endangered or threatened by the State of Illinois. The site offers a wide array of recreation opportunities, including hiking, biking, canoeing, fishing and seasonal hunting programs.

Check In:............................. Check Out:...............................

Lodging:................................. Park hours:........................

Who I Went With:..

Fee(s):................................. Will I Return?   YES / NO

Rating ⭐ ⭐ ⭐ ⭐ ⭐

Activities

❑ ATV/OHV	❑ Horseback Riding	❑ Fishing	❑ Wildlife
❑ Berry Picking	❑ Kayaking	❑ Hiking	❑ Bird Viewing
❑ Biking	❑ Photography	❑ Hunting	❑ Snowmobiling
❑ Boating	❑ Skiing	❑ Snowshoeing	❑ ....
❑ Canoeing	❑ Skijoring	❑ Swimming	❑ ....

Facilities

❑ ADA	❑ Visitor Center	❑ Museum	❑ ....
❑ Gift Shop	❑ Picnic Sites	❑ Restrooms	❑ ....

Notes

....
....
....
....

Passport Stamps

CAPE BEND STATE FISH AND WILDLIFE AREA

Alexander

DATE(S) VISITED:..

❑ SPRING ❑ SUMMER ❑ FALL ❑ WINTER

WEATHER	TEMP:
☀ ❄☁ ☁ ☁|||||| ☁☔ ☁	
❑ ❑ ❑ ❑ ❑ ❑	

Check In:............................. Check Out:.............................

Lodging:.................................. Park hours:........................

Who I Went With:...

Fee(s):.. Will I Return? YES / NO

Rating ⭐⭐⭐⭐⭐

ABOUT THIS STATE PARK

Approximately 2,050 acres at the south end of the main site are designated as a Public Hunting Area. Goose and duck hunting is on a permit basis with goose permits (allowing either species to be hunted). Some rental decoys and transportation to the field provided on the area. A total of 35 blinds can accommodate 70 hunters each day.

Activities

❑ ATV/OHV	❑ Horseback Riding	❑ Fishing	❑ Wildlife
❑ Berry Picking	❑ Kayaking	❑ Hiking	❑ Bird Viewing
❑ Biking	❑ Photography	❑ Hunting	❑ Snowmobiling
❑ Boating	❑ Skiing	❑ Snowshoeing	❑ ....
❑ Canoeing	❑ Skijoring	❑ Swimming	❑ ....

Facilities

❑ ADA	❑ Visitor Center	❑ Museum	❑ ....
❑ Gift Shop	❑ Picnic Sites	❑ Restrooms	❑ ....

Notes

....
....
....
....

Passport Stamps

CARLYLE LAKE STATE FISH AND WILDLIFE AREA

Fayette

DATE(S) VISITED:...

❑ SPRING   ❑ SUMMER   ❑ FALL   ❑ WINTER

WEATHER	TEMP:

❑   ❑   ❑   ❑   ❑   ❑

ABOUT THIS STATE PARK

A tremendous variety of outdoor recreational opportunities and natural beauty awaits you at Carlyle Lake State Fish & Wildlife Area. The area is at the northern end of Carlyle Lake and at the southwestern tip of Fayette County. Recreational opportunities abound on the lake and at Eldon Hazlet State Park, at the southern end of the lake. At the Fish and Wildlife Area, however, the pleasures are simple and revolve mainly around enjoying the beauty and solitude of nature as visitors birdwatch, fish and hunt.

Check In:............................. Check Out:.............................

Lodging:................................. Park hours:........................

Who I Went With:...

Fee(s):... Will I Return?   YES / NO

Rating ★ ★ ★ ★ ★

Activities

❑ ATV/OHV   ❑ Horseback Riding   ❑ Fishing   ❑ Wildlife
❑ Berry Picking   ❑ Kayaking   ❑ Hiking   ❑ Bird Viewing
❑ Biking   ❑ Photography   ❑ Hunting   ❑ Snowmobiling
❑ Boating   ❑ Skiing   ❑ Snowshoeing   ❑ ....
❑ Canoeing   ❑ Skijoring   ❑ Swimming   ❑ ....

Facilities

❑ ADA   ❑ Visitor Center   ❑ Museum   ❑ ....
❑ Gift Shop   ❑ Picnic Sites   ❑ Restrooms   ❑ ....

Notes

....
....
....
....

Passport Stamps

CASTLE ROCK STATE PARK

Ogle

DATE(S) VISITED:...

❑ SPRING   ❑ SUMMER   ❑ FALL   ❑ WINTER

ABOUT THIS STATE PARK

WEATHER	TEMP:

❑ ☀ ❑ ⛅ ❑ ☁ ❑ 🌧 ❑ 🌨 ❑ 🌨

Castle Rock State Park is located along the west bank of the Rock River in Ogle County, three miles south of Oregon, on Ill. Rt. 2. The park is centrally located in the Rock River Hills region of Illinois, and its rolling topography is drained by the Rock River. The park is representative of the Rock River Hills area with rock formations, ravines and unique northern plant associations. A sandstone bluff, adjacent to the river, has given the park its name.

Check In:............................ Check Out:............................

Lodging:................................ Park hours:............................

Who I Went With:..

Fee(s):.. Will I Return?   YES / NO

Rating
⭐ ⭐ ⭐ ⭐ ⭐

Activities

❑ ATV/OHV	❑ Horseback Riding	❑ Fishing	❑ Wildlife
❑ Berry Picking	❑ Kayaking	❑ Hiking	❑ Bird Viewing
❑ Biking	❑ Photography	❑ Hunting	❑ Snowmobiling
❑ Boating	❑ Skiing	❑ Snowshoeing	❑ ....
❑ Canoeing	❑ Skijoring	❑ Swimming	❑ ....

Facilities

❑ ADA	❑ Visitor Center	❑ Museum	❑ ....
❑ Gift Shop	❑ Picnic Sites	❑ Restrooms	❑ ....

Notes
....
....
....
....

Passport Stamps

CAVE-IN-ROCK STATE PARK

Hardin

DATE(S) VISITED:..

❏ SPRING   ❏ SUMMER   ❏ FALL   ❏ WINTER

WEATHER	TEMP:
☀ ❏ ✴☁ ❏ ☁ ❏ 🌧 ❏ 🌨 ❏ 🌦 ❏	

ABOUT THIS STATE PARK

At Cave-In-Rock in southern Illinois, atop the high bluffs overlooking the scenic Ohio River, the heavily wooded park is named for the 55-foot-wide cave that was carved out of the limestone rock by water thousands of years ago. The park contains hiking trails of moderate difficulty for exploration and appreciation of tranquil forests and inspiring views. A pond is available for fishing, and the Ohio River provides excellent fishing, boating and water sport opportunities. The river can be accessed directly from two boat ramps.

Check In:............................ Check Out:..............................

Lodging:................................ Park hours:......................

Who I Went With:..

Fee(s):.................................... Will I Return?   YES / NO

Rating ★ ★ ★ ★ ★

Activities

❏ ATV/OHV	❏ Horseback Riding	❏ Fishing	❏ Wildlife
❏ Berry Picking	❏ Kayaking	❏ Hiking	❏ Bird Viewing
❏ Biking	❏ Photography	❏ Hunting	❏ Snowmobiling
❏ Boating	❏ Skiing	❏ Snowshoeing	❏ ....
❏ Canoeing	❏ Skijoring	❏ Swimming	❏ ....

Facilities

❏ ADA	❏ Visitor Center	❏ Museum	❏ ....
❏ Gift Shop	❏ Picnic Sites	❏ Restrooms	❏ ....

Notes

....
....
....
....

Passport Stamps

CHAIN O'LAKES STATE PARK   McHenry

DATE(S) VISITED:...

☐ SPRING ☐ SUMMER ☐ FALL ☐ WINTER

WEATHER	TEMP:
☀ ☁ ☁ ☁ ☁ ☁	
☐ ☐ ☐ ☐ ☐ ☐	

Check In:............................ Check Out:............................

Lodging:.................................. Park hours:.....................

Who I Went With:..

Fee(s):.. Will I Return? YES / NO

Rating ★ ★ ★ ★ ★

ABOUT THIS STATE PARK

Located in the heart of Illinois' largest concentration of natural lakes, Chain O'Lakes State Park is a water-oriented recreation area with outstanding opportunities for boaters, anglers and skiers. the park contains a 44-acre lake within its boundaries. With nearly 6,500 acres of water and 488 miles of shoreline, Chain O'Lakes State Park is the heart of a water wonderland. The park also contains 8 miles of equestrian trail and a 6 miles biking/hiking trail. Camping is popular at Chain O'Lakes.

Activities

☐ ATV/OHV   ☐ Horseback Riding   ☐ Fishing   ☐ Wildlife

☐ Berry Picking   ☐ Kayaking   ☐ Hiking   ☐ Bird Viewing

☐ Biking   ☐ Photography   ☐ Hunting   ☐ Snowmobiling

☐ Boating   ☐ Skiing   ☐ Snowshoeing   ☐ ....

☐ Canoeing   ☐ Skijoring   ☐ Swimming   ☐ ....

Facilities

☐ ADA   ☐ Visitor Center   ☐ Museum   ☐ ....

☐ Gift Shop   ☐ Picnic Sites   ☐ Restrooms   ☐ ....

Notes

....
....
....
....

Passport Stamps

CHANNAHON STATE PARK

Will

DATE(S) VISITED:..

❏ SPRING   ❏ SUMMER   ❏ FALL   ❏ WINTER

WEATHER						TEMP:
☀	☁	☁	☔	☁	☁	
❏	❏	❏	❏	❏	❏	

Check In:................................ Check Out:................................

Lodging:.................................... Park hours:......................

Who I Went With:..

Fee(s):.. Will I Return?   YES / NO

Rating ⭐ ⭐ ⭐ ⭐ ⭐

ABOUT THIS STATE PARK

Channahon State Park is the official trailhead for the Illinois & Michigan Canal State Trail. Channahon is an Indian word meaning "the meeting of the waters" and signifies the joining of the DuPage, Des Plaines and Kankakee rivers. Today, Channahon State Park is under the management of the Illinois Department of Natural Resources and provides park visitors a look back at a historic waterway that transformed a state.

Activities

❏ ATV/OHV	❏ Horseback Riding	❏ Fishing	❏ Wildlife
❏ Berry Picking	❏ Kayaking	❏ Hiking	❏ Bird Viewing
❏ Biking	❏ Photography	❏ Hunting	❏ Snowmobiling
❏ Boating	❏ Skiing	❏ Snowshoeing	❏ ....
❏ Canoeing	❏ Skijoring	❏ Swimming	❏ ....

Facilities

❏ ADA	❏ Visitor Center	❏ Museum	❏ ....
❏ Gift Shop	❏ Picnic Sites	❏ Restrooms	❏ ....

Notes

....

....

....

....

Passport Stamps

CLINTON LAKE STATE RECREATION AREA | DeWitt

DATE(S) VISITED:...

❑ SPRING   ❑ SUMMER   ❑ FALL   ❑ WINTER

WEATHER	TEMP:

☀ ❄☁ ☁ 🌧 ⛈ 🌨
❑ ❑ ❑ ❑ ❑ ❑

ABOUT THIS STATE PARK

The 4,900-acre lake and outstanding fishing are the primary draws, with accessible boat launches at the Mascoutin and West Side Access Areas, a fishing pier at the Spillway Access Area, and bank fishing at Valley Mill. From crappie to catfish to bass and walleye - anglers love Clinton Lake. Hiking trails throughout the site and along the lake shoreline range from easy to moderate in difficulty. Picnic areas and playgrounds are found throughout the site.

Check In:.............................. Check Out:..............................

Lodging:.................................... Park hours:.......................

Who I Went With:..

Fee(s):.. Will I Return?   YES / NO

Rating ⭐ ⭐ ⭐ ⭐ ⭐

Activities

❑ ATV/OHV   ❑ Horseback Riding   ❑ Fishing   ❑ Wildlife
❑ Berry Picking   ❑ Kayaking   ❑ Hiking   ❑ Bird Viewing
❑ Biking   ❑ Photography   ❑ Hunting   ❑ Snowmobiling
❑ Boating   ❑ Skiing   ❑ Snowshoeing   ❑ ....
❑ Canoeing   ❑ Skijoring   ❑ Swimming   ❑ ....

Facilities

❑ ADA   ❑ Visitor Center   ❑ Museum   ❑ ....
❑ Gift Shop   ❑ Picnic Sites   ❑ Restrooms   ❑ ....

Notes

....
....
....
....

Passport Stamps

COFFEEN LAKE STATE FISH AND WILDLIFE AREA

Montgomery

DATE(S) VISITED:..

❏ SPRING   ❏ SUMMER   ❏ FALL   ❏ WINTER

WEATHER	TEMP:

❏ ❏ ❏ ❏ ❏ ❏

ABOUT THIS STATE PARK

Coffeen Lake is an attractive site with a history of providing anglers and hunters great success. The site was opened in 1986 and operates under a long-term lease and management agreement between the Illinois Department of Natural Resources and Ameren Energy Generating Company. This agreement grants authority to the State of Illinois to open the lake and certain lands to the public for recreational activities, such as fishing, boating, picnicking and hunting.

Check In:.............................. Check Out:..............................

Lodging:................................ Park hours:........................

Who I Went With:...

Fee(s):... Will I Return?   YES / NO

Rating ★ ★ ★ ★ ★

Activities

❏ ATV/OHV
❏ Berry Picking
❏ Biking
❏ Boating
❏ Canoeing

❏ Horseback Riding
❏ Kayaking
❏ Photography
❏ Skiing
❏ Skijoring

❏ Fishing
❏ Hiking
❏ Hunting
❏ Snowshoeing
❏ Swimming

❏ Wildlife
❏ Bird Viewing
❏ Snowmobiling
❏ ....
❏ ....

Facilities

❏ ADA
❏ Gift Shop

❏ Visitor Center
❏ Picnic Sites

❏ Museum
❏ Restrooms

❏ ....
❏ ....

Notes

....
....
....
....

Passport Stamps

CRAWFORD COUNTY STATE FISH AND WILDLIFE AREA

Crawford

DATE(S) VISITED:..

☐ SPRING   ☐ SUMMER   ☐ FALL   ☐ WINTER

ABOUT THIS STATE PARK

WEATHER			TEMP:		
☀	☁	☁	☁	☁	☁
☐	☐	☐	☐	☐	☐

Being roughly bisected from east to west by Hutson Creek, the area is generally rolling. South of the creek is more steeply rolling, and forms a bluff. About 100 acres of bottomland are located adjacent to the creek, mostly on the north side of the stream. Some open land is farmed to improve wildlife habitat and insure abundant, good quality grain foods for game and other wildlife species. The forested areas are high quality mature oak-hickory type.

Check In:............................. Check Out:.............................

Lodging:................................ Park hours:..............................

Who I Went With:..

Fee(s):.. Will I Return?   YES / NO

Rating ★ ★ ★ ★ ★

Activities

☐ ATV/OHV   ☐ Horseback Riding   ☐ Fishing   ☐ Wildlife
☐ Berry Picking ☐ Kayaking   ☐ Hiking   ☐ Bird Viewing
☐ Biking   ☐ Photography   ☐ Hunting   ☐ Snowmobiling
☐ Boating   ☐ Skiing   ☐ Snowshoeing   ☐ ....
☐ Canoeing   ☐ Skijoring   ☐ Swimming   ☐ ....

Facilities

☐ ADA   ☐ Visitor Center   ☐ Museum   ☐ ....
☐ Gift Shop   ☐ Picnic Sites   ☐ Restrooms   ☐ ....

Notes
....
....
....
....

Passport Stamps

DELABAR STATE PARK

Henderson

DATE(S) VISITED:..

❑ SPRING   ❑ SUMMER   ❑ FALL   ❑ WINTER

WEATHER	TEMP:
☀ ❑ ❋☁ ❑ ☁ ❑ ☁🌧 ❑ ☁❄ ❑ ☁ ❑	

Check In:............................ Check Out:...............................

Lodging:................................. Park hours:........................

Who I Went With:..

Fee(s):... Will I Return?   YES / NO

Rating   ★ ★ ★ ★ ★

ABOUT THIS STATE PARK

Many of the Henderson County park's 89 acres are forested with sturdy oaks, along with some birch and hickory trees. These forested areas serve as natural habitat for a variety of wildlife species . More than 50 species of birds have been identified in the park, making Delabar State Park a natural haven for birders from throughout the state. The park is named to honor two brothers, Roy and Jack Delabar, who donated the site to the state in 1959 to be developed as a state park. The park officially opened in 1960.

Activities

❑ ATV/OHV	❑ Horseback Riding	❑ Fishing	❑ Wildlife
❑ Berry Picking	❑ Kayaking	❑ Hiking	❑ Bird Viewing
❑ Biking	❑ Photography	❑ Hunting	❑ Snowmobiling
❑ Boating	❑ Skiing	❑ Snowshoeing	❑ ....
❑ Canoeing	❑ Skijoring	❑ Swimming	❑ ....

Facilities

❑ ADA	❑ Visitor Center	❑ Museum	❑ ....
❑ Gift Shop	❑ Picnic Sites	❑ Restrooms	❑ ....

Notes

....
....
....
....

Passport Stamps

DES PLAINES FISH AND WILDLIFE AREA　　Will

DATE(S) VISITED:...

❏ SPRING　　❏ SUMMER　　❏ FALL　　❏ WINTER

| WEATHER | TEMP: |

☀ ❄☁ ☁ 🌧 🌨 🌨
❏　　❏　　❏　　❏　　❏　　❏

ABOUT THIS STATE PARK

A tranquil setting, flowing rivers and natural prairie land - the Des Plaines Fish and Wildlife Area has it all. Visitors will delight in the abundance of wildlife, restful picnic areas and variety of sportfishing species. Farmland and woodland, prairie and swamp, still water and shoreline offer unlimited opportunities for nature lovers and sportsmen. More than 350,000 people annually visit Des Plaines SFWA - an area of more than 5,000 acres, including approximately 200 acres of water.

Check In:.............................. Check Out:..............................

Lodging:.................................. Park hours:........................

Who I Went With:...

Fee(s):... Will I Return?　YES / NO

Rating　⭐ ⭐ ⭐ ⭐ ⭐

Activities

❏ ATV/OHV
❏ Berry Picking
❏ Biking
❏ Boating
❏ Canoeing

❏ Horseback Riding
❏ Kayaking
❏ Photography
❏ Skiing
❏ Skijoring

❏ Fishing
❏ Hiking
❏ Hunting
❏ Snowshoeing
❏ Swimming

❏ Wildlife
❏ Bird Viewing
❏ Snowmobiling
❏ ....
❏ ....

Facilities

❏ ADA
❏ Gift Shop

❏ Visitor Center
❏ Picnic Sites

❏ Museum
❏ Restrooms

❏ ....
❏ ....

Notes

....
....
....
....

Passport Stamps

DIXON SPRINGS STATE PARK

Pope

DATE(S) VISITED:..

❏ SPRING ❏ SUMMER ❏ FALL ❏ WINTER

WEATHER	TEMP:

❏ ❏ ❏ ❏ ❏ ❏

Check In:............................. Check Out:...............................

Lodging:.................................... Park hours:........................

Who I Went With:..

Fee(s):... Will I Return? YES / NO

Rating ★ ★ ★ ★ ★

ABOUT THIS STATE PARK

Dixon Springs State Park is one of several state parks in the Illinois Shawnee Hills. The park is situated on a giant block of sandstone deposited 315 million years ago, which was dropped 500 feet along a fault line that extends northwesterly across Pope County. The resulting rocky scenery gives visitors the chance to explore breathtaking canyons and waterfalls.

Activities

❏ ATV/OHV	❏ Horseback Riding	❏ Fishing	❏ Wildlife
❏ Berry Picking	❏ Kayaking	❏ Hiking	❏ Bird Viewing
❏ Biking	❏ Photography	❏ Hunting	❏ Snowmobiling
❏ Boating	❏ Skiing	❏ Snowshoeing	❏ ....
❏ Canoeing	❏ Skijoring	❏ Swimming	❏ ....

Facilities

❏ ADA	❏ Visitor Center	❏ Museum	❏ ....
❏ Gift Shop	❏ Picnic Sites	❏ Restrooms	❏ ....

Notes

....
....
....
....

Passport Stamps

DONNELLEY/DEPUE STATE PARK

Putnam

DATE(S) VISITED:...

❑ SPRING   ❑ SUMMER   ❑ FALL   ❑ WINTER

WEATHER	TEMP:
☀ ❄🌤 ☁ 🌧 ⛈ 🌨	
❑ ❑ ❑ ❑ ❑ ❑	

Check In:............................. Check Out:...........................

Lodging:............................ Park hours:.......................

Who I Went With:...

Fee(s):... Will I Return?   YES / NO

Rating ⭐ ⭐ ⭐ ⭐ ⭐

ABOUT THIS STATE PARK

he Donnelley/DePue State Fish and Wildlife Areas complex is managed primarily for migratory waterfowl. Frank C. Bellrose, world-renown waterfowl expert, designated this Great Bend as the entry point to the lower Illinois River valley, an important North American waterfowl migration corridor. These state wildlife areas contain a variety of wetland habitats critical to migratory waterfowl. Consequently, much of the 3,015-acre complex is managed for waterfowl feeding, nesting, resting, hunting and viewing.

Activities

❑ ATV/OHV	❑ Horseback Riding	❑ Fishing	❑ Wildlife
❑ Berry Picking	❑ Kayaking	❑ Hiking	❑ Bird Viewing
❑ Biking	❑ Photography	❑ Hunting	❑ Snowmobiling
❑ Boating	❑ Skiing	❑ Snowshoeing	❑ ....
❑ Canoeing	❑ Skijoring	❑ Swimming	❑ ....

Facilities

❑ ADA	❑ Visitor Center	❑ Museum	❑ ....
❑ Gift Shop	❑ Picnic Sites	❑ Restrooms	❑ ....

Notes

....
....
....
....

Passport Stamps

EAGLE CREEK STATE RECREATION AREA

Shelby

DATE(S) VISITED:...

❏ SPRING   ❏ SUMMER   ❏ FALL   ❏ WINTER

WEATHER	TEMP:
☀ ❄☁ ☁ 🌧 ⛈ 🌦	
❏ ❏ ❏ ❏ ❏ ❏	

Check In:............................ Check Out:..............................

Lodging:............................ Park hours:........................

Who I Went With:...

Fee(s):.. Will I Return? YES / NO

Rating ⭐ ⭐ ⭐ ⭐ ⭐

ABOUT THIS STATE PARK

Four miles southeast of Findlay, the Shelby County sites encompass 11,100-acres of water, 250 miles of shoreline and large tracts of carefully maintained indigenous woodland ideal for camping, hiking, horseback riding, snowmobiling, fishing, water skiing, pontoon boating, windsurfing or just plain bobbing and drifting on the glittering expanse of the lake.

Activities

❏ ATV/OHV	❏ Horseback Riding	❏ Fishing	❏ Wildlife
❏ Berry Picking	❏ Kayaking	❏ Hiking	❏ Bird Viewing
❏ Biking	❏ Photography	❏ Hunting	❏ Snowmobiling
❏ Boating	❏ Skiing	❏ Snowshoeing	❏ ....
❏ Canoeing	❏ Skijoring	❏ Swimming	❏ ....

Facilities

❏ ADA	❏ Visitor Center	❏ Museum	❏ ....
❏ Gift Shop	❏ Picnic Sites	❏ Restrooms	❏ ....

Notes

....
....
....
....

Passport Stamps

EDWARD R. MADIGAN STATE FISH AND WILDLIFE AREA

Logan

DATE(S) VISITED:..

❏ SPRING ❏ SUMMER ❏ FALL ❏ WINTER

ABOUT THIS STATE PARK

Edward R. Madigan State Fish and Wildlife Area, a 974-acre site along Salt Creek just south of Lincoln in Logan Co., is an ideal destination for those looking for a quiet and peaceful outdoors experience. The site features opportunities for hiking, biking, canoeing, wildlife watching, fishing, picnics and hunting. The forest canopy of Madigan SFWA includes oak, walnut, sycamore, ash, hackberry, hickory and sycamore; including the largest sycamore tree in Illinois. Native birds and wildlife abound.

WEATHER						TEMP:
❏	❏	❏	❏	❏	❏	

Check In:.............................. Check Out:..............................

Lodging:.................................. Park hours:......................

Who I Went With:..

Fee(s):... Will I Return? YES / NO

Rating ⭐ ⭐ ⭐ ⭐ ⭐

Activities

❏ ATV/OHV   ❏ Horseback Riding   ❏ Fishing   ❏ Wildlife
❏ Berry Picking ❏ Kayaking   ❏ Hiking   ❏ Bird Viewing
❏ Biking   ❏ Photography   ❏ Hunting   ❏ Snowmobiling
❏ Boating   ❏ Skiing   ❏ Snowshoeing ❏ ....
❏ Canoeing   ❏ Skijoring   ❏ Swimming   ❏ ....

Facilities

❏ ADA   ❏ Visitor Center   ❏ Museum   ❏ ....
❏ Gift Shop ❏ Picnic Sites   ❏ Restrooms ❏ ....

Notes

....
....
....
....

Passport Stamps

ELDON HAZLET STATE RECREATION AREA

Clinton

DATE(S) VISITED:..

☐ SPRING ☐ SUMMER ☐ FALL ☐ WINTER

WEATHER	TEMP:
☀ ☀🌤 ☁ 🌧 ⛈ 🌨	
☐ ☐ ☐ ☐ ☐ ☐	

Check In:.............................. Check Out:..............................

Lodging:................................. Park hours:........................

Who I Went With:...

Fee(s):... Will I Return? YES / NO

Rating ⭐ ⭐ ⭐ ⭐ ⭐

ABOUT THIS STATE PARK

Eldon Hazlet State Recreation Area is a 3,000-acre site on the western shore of Carlyle Lake, a Kaskaskia River impoundment. The site is located 3 miles north of Carlyle and 2 miles east of Illinois Route 127 in Clinton County. Eldon Hazlet SRA attracts more than 800,000 visitors annually to camp, boat, fish, hunt, picnic, bird watch and to hike more than 9 miles of trails. Also popular are the sailboat regattas, held almost every summer weekend.

Activities

☐ ATV/OHV   ☐ Horseback Riding   ☐ Fishing   ☐ Wildlife
☐ Berry Picking   ☐ Kayaking   ☐ Hiking   ☐ Bird Viewing
☐ Biking   ☐ Photography   ☐ Hunting   ☐ Snowmobiling
☐ Boating   ☐ Skiing   ☐ Snowshoeing   ☐ ....
☐ Canoeing   ☐ Skijoring   ☐ Swimming   ☐ ....

Facilities

☐ ADA   ☐ Visitor Center   ☐ Museum   ☐ ....
☐ Gift Shop   ☐ Picnic Sites   ☐ Restrooms   ☐ ....

Notes

....

....

....

....

Passport Stamps

FERNE CLYFFE STATE PARK

Johnson

DATE(S) VISITED:...

❑ SPRING   ❑ SUMMER   ❑ FALL   ❑ WINTER

WEATHER	TEMP:
☀ ❑ ☀☁ ❑ ☁ ❑ 🌧 ❑ ❄ ❑ ❑	

ABOUT THIS STATE PARK

Ferne Clyffe State Park has been known as an outstanding natural scenic spot for a century. An abundance of ferns, unique geological features and unusual plant communities create an atmosphere that enhances the many recreational facilities offered at the park. Trails wind through picturesque woods, allowing visitors to view fascinating rock formations and inspiring vistas. Ferne Clyffe also offers camping, picnicking, hiking, hunting and fishing.

Check In:.............................. Check Out:...............................

Lodging:.................................. Park hours:........................

Who I Went With:..

Fee(s):.. Will I Return?   YES / NO

Rating ★ ★ ★ ★ ★

Activities

❑ ATV/OHV   ❑ Horseback Riding   ❑ Fishing   ❑ Wildlife
❑ Berry Picking   ❑ Kayaking   ❑ Hiking   ❑ Bird Viewing
❑ Biking   ❑ Photography   ❑ Hunting   ❑ Snowmobiling
❑ Boating   ❑ Skiing   ❑ Snowshoeing   ❑ ....
❑ Canoeing   ❑ Skijoring   ❑ Swimming   ❑ ....

Facilities

❑ ADA   ❑ Visitor Center   ❑ Museum   ❑ ....
❑ Gift Shop   ❑ Picnic Sites   ❑ Restrooms   ❑ ....

Notes

....
....
....
....

Passport Stamps

FORT MASSAC STATE PARK

Massac

DATE(S) VISITED:...

❏ SPRING ❏ SUMMER ❏ FALL ❏ WINTER

WEATHER			TEMP:		
☀	☁	☁	☁	☁	☁
❏	❏	❏	❏	❏	❏

Check In:............................. Check Out:...............................

Lodging:.................................... Park hours:........................

Who I Went With:...

Fee(s):.. Will I Return? YES / NO

Rating ⭐ ⭐ ⭐ ⭐ ⭐

ABOUT THIS STATE PARK

Fort Massac is a captivating reminder of days gone by, a fascinating excursion through the entire course of American history, and the perfect place to relax in soothing natural surroundings. The nearly 1,500-acre park is perfect for picnics, camping, hiking, fishing, boating, and seasonal hunting programs. The park also has an 18-hole disc golf course. Fort Massac State Park is also home to special events that bring to life Colonial and early American history.

Activities

❏ ATV/OHV	❏ Horseback Riding	❏ Fishing	❏ Wildlife
❏ Berry Picking	❏ Kayaking	❏ Hiking	❏ Bird Viewing
❏ Biking	❏ Photography	❏ Hunting	❏ Snowmobiling
❏ Boating	❏ Skiing	❏ Snowshoeing	❏ ....
❏ Canoeing	❏ Skijoring	❏ Swimming	❏ ....

Facilities

❏ ADA	❏ Visitor Center	❏ Museum	❏ ....
❏ Gift Shop	❏ Picnic Sites	❏ Restrooms	❏ ....

Notes

....
....
....
....

Passport Stamps

FOX RIDGE STATE PARK

Coles

DATE(S) VISITED:...

❑ SPRING　　❑ SUMMER　　❑ FALL　　❑ WINTER

WEATHER				TEMP:	
☀	☁	☁	☁	☁	☁
❑	❑	❑	❑	❑	❑

Check In:............................ Check Out:............................

Lodging:............................ Park hours:.......................

Who I Went With:..

Fee(s):... Will I Return?　YES / NO

Rating　⭐ ⭐ ⭐ ⭐ ⭐

ABOUT THIS STATE PARK

Fox Ridge State Park, a 2,064-acre park just south of Charleston in east-central Illinois, is known for its steep, thickly wooded ridges, broad, lush valleys and miles of rugged, scenic hiking trails. More than 40 campsites and two rustic cabins are available at Fox Ridge. Day use picnic areas are located throughout the park. The northern area of the park contains 1,129 acres open for public hunting.

Activities

❑ ATV/OHV	❑ Horseback Riding	❑ Fishing	❑ Wildlife
❑ Berry Picking	❑ Kayaking	❑ Hiking	❑ Bird Viewing
❑ Biking	❑ Photography	❑ Hunting	❑ Snowmobiling
❑ Boating	❑ Skiing	❑ Snowshoeing	❑ ....
❑ Canoeing	❑ Skijoring	❑ Swimming	❑ ....

Facilities

❑ ADA	❑ Visitor Center	❑ Museum	❑ ....
❑ Gift Shop	❑ Picnic Sites	❑ Restrooms	❑ ....

Notes

....
....
....
....

Passport Stamps

FRANK HOLTEN STATE RECREATION AREA

St. Clair

DATE(S) VISITED:..

❑ SPRING   ❑ SUMMER   ❑ FALL   ❑ WINTER

WEATHER	TEMP:
☀ ❄ ☁ ☁ 🌧 ☁	
❑ ❑ ❑ ❑ ❑ ❑	

Check In:............................. Check Out:.............................

Lodging:.................................... Park hours:.......................

Who I Went With:..

Fee(s):... Will I Return?   YES / NO

Rating ⭐ ⭐ ⭐ ⭐ ⭐

ABOUT THIS STATE PARK

Frank Holten State Recreation Area is an ideal destination for outdoor recreation in an urban setting in East St. Louis. The 1,080-acre St. Clair County park features the 18-hole Grand Marais Golf Course, two lakes for outstanding fishing, and plenty of open space for picnicking and other outdoors fun. The site is named for the late Frank Holten, who served the region in the Illinois General Assembly for 48 years.

Activities

❑ ATV/OHV   ❑ Horseback Riding   ❑ Fishing   ❑ Wildlife

❑ Berry Picking   ❑ Kayaking   ❑ Hiking   ❑ Bird Viewing

❑ Biking   ❑ Photography   ❑ Hunting   ❑ Snowmobiling

❑ Boating   ❑ Skiing   ❑ Snowshoeing   ❑ ....

❑ Canoeing   ❑ Skijoring   ❑ Swimming   ❑ ....

Facilities

❑ ADA   ❑ Visitor Center   ❑ Museum   ❑ ....

❑ Gift Shop   ❑ Picnic Sites   ❑ Restrooms   ❑ ....

Notes

....

....

....

....

Passport Stamps

FRANKLIN CREEK STATE NATURAL AREA

Lee

DATE(S) VISITED:..

☐ SPRING ☐ SUMMER ☐ FALL ☐ WINTER

ABOUT THIS STATE PARK

Franklin Creek State Natural Area is located in Lee County, northwest of the village of Franklin Grove and east of Dixon just north of IL Rt. 38. Beautiful Franklin Creek flows throughout the 882-acre park. Several large natural springs, hardwood forests, bedrock outcroppings and a large variety of flora and fauna comprise a pristine ecosystem. Hiking and seasonal cross country skiing and snowmobile trails, along with equestrian trails, are popular destinations for site visitors.

WEATHER			TEMP:		
☐	☐	☐	☐	☐	☐

Check In:............................. Check Out:.............................

Lodging:.................................. Park hours:.......................

Who I Went With:..

Fee(s):.. Will I Return? YES / NO

Rating ⭐ ⭐ ⭐ ⭐ ⭐

Activities

☐ ATV/OHV
☐ Berry Picking
☐ Biking
☐ Boating
☐ Canoeing

☐ Horseback Riding
☐ Kayaking
☐ Photography
☐ Skiing
☐ Skijoring

☐ Fishing
☐ Hiking
☐ Hunting
☐ Snowshoeing
☐ Swimming

☐ Wildlife
☐ Bird Viewing
☐ Snowmobiling
☐ ....
☐ ....

Facilities

☐ ADA
☐ Gift Shop

☐ Visitor Center
☐ Picnic Sites

☐ Museum
☐ Restrooms

☐ ....
☐ ....

Notes

....
....
....
....

Passport Stamps

DATE(S) VISITED:..

☐ SPRING ☐ SUMMER ☐ FALL ☐ WINTER

WEATHER	TEMP:

☀ ❄☁ ☁ 🌧 🌨 🌦
☐ ☐ ☐ ☐ ☐ ☐

Check In:............................. Check Out:...............................

Lodging:..................................... Park hours:........................

Who I Went With:...

Fee(s):.. Will I Return? YES / NO

Rating ⭐ ⭐ ⭐ ⭐ ⭐

ABOUT THIS STATE PARK

The 997-acre Fults Hill Prairie State Natural Area is owned and managed by the Illinois Department of Natural Resources. Most of this unique natural area was purchased between 1970 and 1976. From the uplands of Fults Hill Prairie Nature Preserve to the lowlands of Kidd Lake Marsh State Natural Area, a variety of plants and animals can be found, some common and some found nowhere else in the state.

Activities

☐ ATV/OHV	☐ Horseback Riding	☐ Fishing	☐ Wildlife
☐ Berry Picking	☐ Kayaking	☐ Hiking	☐ Bird Viewing
☐ Biking	☐ Photography	☐ Hunting	☐ Snowmobiling
☐ Boating	☐ Skiing	☐ Snowshoeing	☐ ....
☐ Canoeing	☐ Skijoring	☐ Swimming	☐ ....

Facilities

☐ ADA	☐ Visitor Center	☐ Museum	☐ ....
☐ Gift Shop	☐ Picnic Sites	☐ Restrooms	☐ ....

Notes

....
....
....
....

Passport Stamps

GEBHARD WOODS STATE PARK

Grundy

DATE(S) VISITED:..

☐ SPRING ☐ SUMMER ☐ FALL ☐ WINTER

WEATHER	TEMP:

☐ ☀ ☐ ❄☁ ☐ ☁ ☐ ☁☂ ☐ ☁ ☐ ☁

Check In:............................. Check Out:.............................

Lodging:................................. Park hours:........................

Who I Went With:..

Fee(s):.. Will I Return? YES / NO

Rating ⭐ ⭐ ⭐ ⭐ ⭐

ABOUT THIS STATE PARK

Hikers, campers, picnickers and canoeists frequent Gebhard Woods State Park, making the 30-acre site one of Illinois' most popular state parks. Located in Morris, this picturesque park is bordered on the south by the Illinois & Michigan Canal and to the north by Nettle Creek, which gently flows along the perimeter and through the park, adding to its natural beauty and abundance of wildlife. Stately old trees including walnut, oak, ash, maple, sycamore, hawthorn and cottonwood provide ample shade throughout the park.

Activities

☐ ATV/OHV   ☐ Horseback Riding ☐ Fishing   ☐ Wildlife
☐ Berry Picking ☐ Kayaking   ☐ Hiking   ☐ Bird Viewing
☐ Biking   ☐ Photography   ☐ Hunting   ☐ Snowmobiling
☐ Boating   ☐ Skiing   ☐ Snowshoeing ☐ ....
☐ Canoeing   ☐ Skijoring   ☐ Swimming   ☐ ....

Facilities

☐ ADA   ☐ Visitor Center ☐ Museum   ☐ ....
☐ Gift Shop ☐ Picnic Sites   ☐ Restrooms ☐ ....

Notes

....
....
....
....

Passport Stamps

GIANT CITY STATE PARK

Jackson, Union

DATE(S) VISITED:...

❑ SPRING   ❑ SUMMER   ❑ FALL   ❑ WINTER

WEATHER		TEMP:			
☀	❆☁	☁	☁⁞⁞⁞⁞	☁ ⚡	☁ ❄
❑	❑	❑	❑	❑	❑

ABOUT THIS STATE PARK

With its breathtaking natural beauty and unlimited opportunities for outdoor recreation, a trip to Giant City State Park near Carbondale is sure to delight visitors of all ages. From camping and horseback riding to fishing and rappelling, it's an outdoor lover's paradise. Visitors will marvel at the many hiking trails. Especially popular is the Giant City Nature Trail, home of the "Giant City Streets" - huge bluffs of sandstone formed 12,000 years ago.

Check In:.............................. Check Out:................................

Lodging:.. Park hours:.........................

Who I Went With:..

Fee(s):.. Will I Return?   YES / NO

Rating   ★ ★ ★ ★ ★

Activities

❑ ATV/OHV	❑ Horseback Riding	❑ Fishing	❑ Wildlife
❑ Berry Picking	❑ Kayaking	❑ Hiking	❑ Bird Viewing
❑ Biking	❑ Photography	❑ Hunting	❑ Snowmobiling
❑ Boating	❑ Skiing	❑ Snowshoeing	❑ ....
❑ Canoeing	❑ Skijoring	❑ Swimming	❑ ....

Facilities

❑ ADA	❑ Visitor Center	❑ Museum	❑ ....
❑ Gift Shop	❑ Picnic Sites	❑ Restrooms	❑ ....

Notes

....
....
....
....

Passport Stamps

GOLCONDA MARINA STATE RECREATION AREA

DATE(S) VISITED:..

❏ SPRING   ❏ SUMMER   ❏ FALL   ❏ WINTER

WEATHER	TEMP:
☀ ❄☁ ☁ ☁ ☁ ☁	
❏ ❏ ❏ ❏ ❏ ❏	

ABOUT THIS STATE PARK

Golconda Marina is located in the southeastern portion of Pope County along a scenic stretch of the Ohio River at Golconda. The 274-acre site is a full-service boat marina with 206 slips. The marina serves as the gateway to the Smithland Pool area of the Ohio River. Smithland Pool, a 23,000-acre recreational area of fingered tributaries off the Ohio River, is recognized as one of the finest fishing and boating areas in the nation.

Check In:............................ Check Out:............................

Lodging:.................................. Park hours:........................

Who I Went With:..

Fee(s):.. Will I Return?   YES / NO

Rating   ★ ★ ★ ★ ★

Activities

❏ ATV/OHV
❏ Berry Picking
❏ Biking
❏ Boating
❏ Canoeing

❏ Horseback Riding
❏ Kayaking
❏ Photography
❏ Skiing
❏ Skijoring

❏ Fishing
❏ Hiking
❏ Hunting
❏ Snowshoeing
❏ Swimming

❏ Wildlife
❏ Bird Viewing
❏ Snowmobiling
❏ ....
❏ ....

Facilities

❏ ADA
❏ Gift Shop

❏ Visitor Center
❏ Picnic Sites

❏ Museum
❏ Restrooms

❏ ....
❏ ....

Notes

....
....
....
....

Passport Stamps

GOOSE LAKE PRAIRIE STATE NATURAL AREA

Grundy

DATE(S) VISITED:..

❑ SPRING ❑ SUMMER ❑ FALL ❑ WINTER

WEATHER	TEMP:

❑ ❑ ❑ ❑ ❑ ❑

Check In:................................ Check Out:...............................

Lodging:.................................. Park hours:........................

Who I Went With:..

Fee(s):.. Will I Return? YES / NO

Rating ⭐ ⭐ ⭐ ⭐ ⭐

ABOUT THIS STATE PARK

Located in Grundy County, Goose Lake Prairie is approximately 50 miles southwest of Chicago and one mile southwest of the confluence of the Kankakee and Des Plaines rivers. More than half of Goose Lake Prairie is a dedicated nature preserve, protected by law for future generations from any change to the natural environment. In addition to furnishing a look into Illinois' past, the prairie provides important nesting habitat for endangered or threatened birds.

Activities

❑ ATV/OHV
❑ Berry Picking
❑ Biking
❑ Boating
❑ Canoeing

❑ Horseback Riding
❑ Kayaking
❑ Photography
❑ Skiing
❑ Skijoring

❑ Fishing
❑ Hiking
❑ Hunting
❑ Snowshoeing
❑ Swimming

❑ Wildlife
❑ Bird Viewing
❑ Snowmobiling
❑ ....
❑ ....

Facilities

❑ ADA
❑ Gift Shop

❑ Visitor Center
❑ Picnic Sites

❑ Museum
❑ Restrooms

❑ ....
❑ ....

Notes

....
....
....
....

Passport Stamps

GREEN RIVER STATE WILDLIFE AREA

Lee

DATE(S) VISITED:...

☐ SPRING ☐ SUMMER ☐ FALL ☐ WINTER

WEATHER	TEMP:
☐ ☐ ☐ ☐ ☐ ☐	

Check In:............................. Check Out:.............................

Lodging:................................. Park hours:.......................

Who I Went With:...

Fee(s):... Will I Return? YES / NO

Rating ⭐ ⭐ ⭐ ⭐ ⭐

ABOUT THIS STATE PARK

The Green River State Wildlife Area is a wildlife restoration area popular among hunters, hikers, birders and other outdoor enthusiasts. Topography of the 2,565-acre area varies from flat to gently rolling. Swampy slough areas dominate nearly a third of the acreage. Many of these areas are planted and managed to provide more food and cover for wildlife. Native prairie plants are found in many portions of the Green River State Wildlife Area.

Activities

☐ ATV/OHV	☐ Horseback Riding	☐ Fishing	☐ Wildlife
☐ Berry Picking	☐ Kayaking	☐ Hiking	☐ Bird Viewing
☐ Biking	☐ Photography	☐ Hunting	☐ Snowmobiling
☐ Boating	☐ Skiing	☐ Snowshoeing	☐ ....
☐ Canoeing	☐ Skijoring	☐ Swimming	☐ ....

Facilities

☐ ADA	☐ Visitor Center	☐ Museum	☐ ....
☐ Gift Shop	☐ Picnic Sites	☐ Restrooms	☐ ....

Notes

....

....

....

....

Passport Stamps

HAMILTON COUNTY STATE FISH AND WILDLIFE AREA

Hamilton

DATE(S) VISITED:..

❏ SPRING   ❏ SUMMER   ❏ FALL   ❏ WINTER

WEATHER			TEMP:		
☀	❄☁	☁	🌧	⛈	🌨
❏	❏	❏	❏	❏	❏

Check In:............................ Check Out:..............................

Lodging:.................................. Park hours:........................

Who I Went With:..

Fee(s):.. Will I Return?   YES / NO

Rating ★ ★ ★ ★ ★

ABOUT THIS STATE PARK

Hamilton County State Fish and Wildlife Area, also known as Dolan Lake. Dolan Lake is the main attraction of the park. The earthen dam was constructed in 1962 and the lake was filled shortly thereafter. The 75-acre lake has 3 miles of shoreline and a maximum depth of 18 feet. The lake contains largemouth bass, bluegill, sunfish, crappie, channel catfish and bullheads. A launching ramp is available. Motors are limited to 10 HP.

Activities

❏ ATV/OHV	❏ Horseback Riding	❏ Fishing	❏ Wildlife
❏ Berry Picking	❏ Kayaking	❏ Hiking	❏ Bird Viewing
❏ Biking	❏ Photography	❏ Hunting	❏ Snowmobiling
❏ Boating	❏ Skiing	❏ Snowshoeing	❏ ....
❏ Canoeing	❏ Skijoring	❏ Swimming	❏ ....

Facilities

❏ ADA	❏ Visitor Center	❏ Museum	❏ ....
❏ Gift Shop	❏ Picnic Sites	❏ Restrooms	❏ ....

Notes

....
....
....
....

Passport Stamps

HARRY "BABE" WOODYARD STATE NATURAL AREA

Vermilion

DATE(S) VISITED:..

❑ SPRING ❑ SUMMER ❑ FALL ❑ WINTER

WEATHER						TEMP:
❑	❑	❑	❑	❑	❑	

Check In:.............................. Check Out:..............................

Lodging:.................................. Park hours:........................

Who I Went With:...

Fee(s):.. Will I Return? YES / NO

Rating ⭐ ⭐ ⭐ ⭐ ⭐

ABOUT THIS STATE PARK

Harry 'Babe' Woodyard State Natural Area is located in scenic rural Vermilion County. The majority of this natural area's 1,104 acres is covered with lush forest. Within the nature area are 12 species that are found on the Illinois Endangered or Threatened Species List. Harry 'Babe' Woodyard State Natural Area is a sportsman's paradise with activities such as fishing, hunting, and hiking.

Activities

❑ ATV/OHV
❑ Berry Picking
❑ Biking
❑ Boating
❑ Canoeing

❑ Horseback Riding
❑ Kayaking
❑ Photography
❑ Skiing
❑ Skijoring

❑ Fishing
❑ Hiking
❑ Hunting
❑ Snowshoeing
❑ Swimming

❑ Wildlife
❑ Bird Viewing
❑ Snowmobiling
❑ ....
❑ ....

Facilities

❑ ADA
❑ Gift Shop

❑ Visitor Center
❑ Picnic Sites

❑ Museum
❑ Restrooms

❑ ....
❑ ....

Notes

....
....
....
....

Passport Stamps

HEIDECKE LAKE STATE FISH & WILDLIFE AREA

Grundy

DATE(S) VISITED:..

❑ SPRING ❑ SUMMER ❑ FALL ❑ WINTER

WEATHER	TEMP:
☀ ❄☁ ☁ ☁(rain) ☁(snow) ☁(drizzle)	
❑ ❑ ❑ ❑ ❑ ❑	

ABOUT THIS STATE PARK

Located southeast of Morris, Heidecke Lake State Fish and Wildlife Area is managed by the Department of Natural Resources for fishing and hunting. DNR has leased Heidecke Lake since 1978, when it was built as a cooling lake for the Collins Power Plant, which now is owned and operated by Midwest Generation. The lake provides more than 1,300 acres of prime fishing opportunities.

Check In:............................. Check Out:.............................

Lodging:.................................. Park hours:.......................

Who I Went With:...

Fee(s):.. Will I Return? YES / NO

Rating ★ ★ ★ ★ ★

Activities

❑ ATV/OHV	❑ Horseback Riding	❑ Fishing	❑ Wildlife
❑ Berry Picking	❑ Kayaking	❑ Hiking	❑ Bird Viewing
❑ Biking	❑ Photography	❑ Hunting	❑ Snowmobiling
❑ Boating	❑ Skiing	❑ Snowshoeing	❑ ....
❑ Canoeing	❑ Skijoring	❑ Swimming	❑ ....

Facilities

❑ ADA	❑ Visitor Center	❑ Museum	❑ ....
❑ Gift Shop	❑ Picnic Sites	❑ Restrooms	❑ ....

Notes

....

....

....

....

Passport Stamps

HENDERSON COUNTY CONSERVATION AREA — Henderson

DATE(S) VISITED:..

❑ SPRING   ❑ SUMMER   ❑ FALL   ❑ WINTER

WEATHER	TEMP:
☀ ❄☁ ☁ 🌧 ☁⚡ ☁❄	
❑ ❑ ❑ ❑ ❑ ❑	

Check In:............................ Check Out:............................

Lodging:................................. Park hours:......................

Who I Went With:..

Fee(s):... Will I Return?   YES / NO

Rating ⭐⭐⭐⭐⭐

ABOUT THIS STATE PARK

Henderson County Conservation Area, which includes Gladstone Lake, offers a variety of recreational facilities. The 27-acre lake has a shoreline of 1.5 miles and a maximum depth of 25 feet. The area, about 20 miles southwest of Monmouth and five miles east of the Mississippi River, has a total of 87 acres.

Activities

❑ ATV/OHV   ❑ Horseback Riding   ❑ Fishing   ❑ Wildlife
❑ Berry Picking   ❑ Kayaking   ❑ Hiking   ❑ Bird Viewing
❑ Biking   ❑ Photography   ❑ Hunting   ❑ Snowmobiling
❑ Boating   ❑ Skiing   ❑ Snowshoeing   ❑ ....
❑ Canoeing   ❑ Skijoring   ❑ Swimming   ❑ ....

Facilities

❑ ADA   ❑ Visitor Center   ❑ Museum   ❑ ....
❑ Gift Shop   ❑ Picnic Sites   ❑ Restrooms   ❑ ....

Notes

....
....
....
....

Passport Stamps

HENNEPIN CANAL PARKWAY STATE PARK

DATE(S) VISITED:...

❑ SPRING　　❑ SUMMER　　❑ FALL　　❑ WINTER

WEATHER			TEMP:		
❑	❑	❑	❑	❑	❑

Check In:............................. Check Out:.............................

Lodging:.................................. Park hours:........................

Who I Went With:..

Fee(s):.. Will I Return?　YES / NO

Rating　⭐ ⭐ ⭐ ⭐ ⭐

ABOUT THIS STATE PARK

The Hennepin Canal State Trail is an ideal destination for a relaxing day of picnicking, hiking, biking, fishing and old fashioned family fun. There are plenty of picnic tables along the 104.5-mile linear park spanning five Illinois counties (Rock Island, Bureau, Henry, Lee and Whiteside).

Activities

❑ ATV/OHV	❑ Horseback Riding	❑ Fishing	❑ Wildlife
❑ Berry Picking	❑ Kayaking	❑ Hiking	❑ Bird Viewing
❑ Biking	❑ Photography	❑ Hunting	❑ Snowmobiling
❑ Boating	❑ Skiing	❑ Snowshoeing	❑ ....
❑ Canoeing	❑ Skijoring	❑ Swimming	❑ ....

Facilities

❑ ADA	❑ Visitor Center	❑ Museum	❑ ....
❑ Gift Shop	❑ Picnic Sites	❑ Restrooms	❑ ....

Notes

....
....
....
....

Passport Stamps

HIDDEN SPRINGS STATE FOREST

Shelby

DATE(S) VISITED:...

❏ SPRING ❏ SUMMER ❏ FALL ❏ WINTER

WEATHER			TEMP:		
❏	❏	❏	❏	❏	❏

Check In:............................ Check Out:..............................

Lodging:................................ Park hours:.........................

Who I Went With:..

Fee(s):.. Will I Return? YES / NO

Rating ⭐⭐⭐⭐⭐

ABOUT THIS STATE PARK

Hidden Springs State Forest (formerly known as Shelby State Forest) consists of approximately 1,200 acres of land near Clarksburg, 10 miles southeast of Shelbyville in Shelby County. The name Hidden Springs was selected because of the property's seven known springs which were used for drinking water by the early settlers. Over the years these springs have been covered over by natural situation and vegetation (hence the name "Hidden Springs"). Rocky Spring and Quicksand Spring have access trails.

Activities

❏ ATV/OHV	❏ Horseback Riding	❏ Fishing	❏ Wildlife
❏ Berry Picking	❏ Kayaking	❏ Hiking	❏ Bird Viewing
❏ Biking	❏ Photography	❏ Hunting	❏ Snowmobiling
❏ Boating	❏ Skiing	❏ Snowshoeing	❏ ....
❏ Canoeing	❏ Skijoring	❏ Swimming	❏ ....

Facilities

❏ ADA	❏ Visitor Center	❏ Museum	❏ ....
❏ Gift Shop	❏ Picnic Sites	❏ Restrooms	❏ ....

Notes
....
....
....
....

Passport Stamps

HORSESHOE LAKE STATE FISH & WILDLIFE AREA — Alexander

DATE(S) VISITED:..

❏ SPRING   ❏ SUMMER   ❏ FALL   ❏ WINTER

WEATHER			TEMP:		
☀ ❏	⛅ ❏	☁ ❏	🌧 ❏	⛈ ❏	🌨 ❏

Check In:........................... Check Out:...............................

Lodging:.................................. Park hours:........................

Who I Went With:...

Fee(s):... Will I Return? YES / NO

Rating ⭐⭐⭐⭐⭐

ABOUT THIS STATE PARK

As you explore the Horseshoe Lake State Fish & Wildlife Area, you may be reminded of the Deep South. The charm of bald cypress, tupelo gum, swamp cottonwood trees and wild lotus makes the recreational activities at the site even more enjoyable. Located in Alexander County just east of Illinois Route 3, 7 miles north of Cairo, the 10,200 acre area includes a 2,400 acre shallow lake. In addition to taking in the beauty of the natural features of the area, visitors enjoy picnicking, camping, boating, fishing and hunting.

Activities

❏ ATV/OHV   ❏ Horseback Riding   ❏ Fishing   ❏ Wildlife
❏ Berry Picking   ❏ Kayaking   ❏ Hiking   ❏ Bird Viewing
❏ Biking   ❏ Photography   ❏ Hunting   ❏ Snowmobiling
❏ Boating   ❏ Skiing   ❏ Snowshoeing   ❏ ....
❏ Canoeing   ❏ Skijoring   ❏ Swimming   ❏ ....

Facilities

❏ ADA   ❏ Visitor Center   ❏ Museum   ❏ ....
❏ Gift Shop   ❏ Picnic Sites   ❏ Restrooms   ❏ ....

Notes
....
....
....
....

Passport Stamps

HORSESHOE LAKE STATE PARK

Madison

DATE(S) VISITED:..

☐ SPRING ☐ SUMMER ☐ FALL ☐ WINTER

WEATHER			TEMP:		
☐	☐	☐	☐	☐	☐

Check In:............................ Check Out:............................

Lodging:................................. Park hours:......................

Who I Went With:...

Fee(s):... Will I Return? YES / NO

Rating
★ ★ ★ ★ ★

ABOUT THIS STATE PARK

It is approximately 2,960 acres (1,198 ha) and surrounds a large horseshoe shaped lake called Horseshoe Lake. Horseshoe Lake is the second largest natural lake in Illinois taking up approximately 2,400 acres (971 ha) of the 2,960-acre (1,198 ha) park. The park has connections to Madison County Transit's Schoolhouse Trail, which connects to over 85 miles (137 km) of bike trail in Madison County.

Activities

☐ ATV/OHV	☐ Horseback Riding	☐ Fishing	☐ Wildlife
☐ Berry Picking	☐ Kayaking	☐ Hiking	☐ Bird Viewing
☐ Biking	☐ Photography	☐ Hunting	☐ Snowmobiling
☐ Boating	☐ Skiing	☐ Snowshoeing	☐ ....
☐ Canoeing	☐ Skijoring	☐ Swimming	☐ ....

Facilities

☐ ADA	☐ Visitor Center	☐ Museum	☐ ....
☐ Gift Shop	☐ Picnic Sites	☐ Restrooms	☐ ....

Notes

....
....
....
....

Passport Stamps

ILLINI STATE PARK

DATE(S) VISITED:..

❑ SPRING   ❑ SUMMER   ❑ FALL   ❑ WINTER

WEATHER	TEMP:
☀ ❄☁ ☁ 🌧 ☁ ☁	
❑ ❑ ❑ ❑ ❑ ❑	

Check In:.............................. Check Out:................................

Lodging:.................................. Park hours:........................

Who I Went With:...

Fee(s):.. Will I Return?   YES / NO

Rating ★ ★ ★ ★ ★

ABOUT THIS STATE PARK

Named for the native Americans who once inhabited the area. Illini State Park is the type of park you think of when you think of big picnics and family gatherings. With its rustic Civilian Conservation Corps buildings and riverside picnic areas, Illini State Park offers beautiful views and a sense of history not found in many other parks.
River fishing is popular out of Illini State Park, where a boat ramp is available.

Activities

❑ ATV/OHV	❑ Horseback Riding	❑ Fishing	❑ Wildlife
❑ Berry Picking	❑ Kayaking	❑ Hiking	❑ Bird Viewing
❑ Biking	❑ Photography	❑ Hunting	❑ Snowmobiling
❑ Boating	❑ Skiing	❑ Snowshoeing	❑ ....
❑ Canoeing	❑ Skijoring	❑ Swimming	❑ ....

Facilities

❑ ADA	❑ Visitor Center	❑ Museum	❑ ....
❑ Gift Shop	❑ Picnic Sites	❑ Restrooms	❑ ....

Notes

....
....
....
....

Passport Stamps

ILLINOIS CAVERNS STATE NATURAL AREA

Monroe

DATE(S) VISITED:...

❑ SPRING   ❑ SUMMER   ❑ FALL   ❑ WINTER

WEATHER			TEMP:		
☀	⛅	☁	🌧	🌨	🌧
❑	❑	❑	❑	❑	❑

Check In:............................. Check Out:.............................

Lodging:................................. Park hours:........................

Who I Went With:...

Fee(s):.. Will I Return?   YES / NO

Rating ⭐⭐⭐⭐⭐

ABOUT THIS STATE PARK

History buffs, nature lovers and sportsmen will thrill to the sights and sounds of the 96-mile route of the Illinois and Michigan Canal. Along its banks are numerous state parks, restored historical sites, and abundance of wildlife and distinctive landscapes, ranging from bluffs to rolling hills. Visitors can follow the I&M Canal State Trail along the old towpath at Rockdale to LaSalle, experiencing 61.5 miles of scenic views and the Des Plaines and Illinois rivers.

Activities

❑ ATV/OHV	❑ Horseback Riding	❑ Fishing	❑ Wildlife
❑ Berry Picking	❑ Kayaking	❑ Hiking	❑ Bird Viewing
❑ Biking	❑ Photography	❑ Hunting	❑ Snowmobiling
❑ Boating	❑ Skiing	❑ Snowshoeing	❑ ....
❑ Canoeing	❑ Skijoring	❑ Swimming	❑ ....

Facilities

❑ ADA	❑ Visitor Center	❑ Museum	❑ ....
❑ Gift Shop	❑ Picnic Sites	❑ Restrooms	❑ ....

Notes

....
....
....
....

Passport Stamps

IROQUOIS COUNTY STATE WILDLIFE AREA

Iroquois

DATE(S) VISITED:..

❏ SPRING   ❏ SUMMER   ❏ FALL   ❏ WINTER

WEATHER	TEMP:

❏   ❏   ❏   ❏   ❏   ❏

Check In:............................. Check Out:.............................

Lodging:.................................. Park hours:........................

Who I Went With:...

Fee(s):....................................... Will I Return?   YES / NO

Rating ★ ★ ★ ★ ★

ABOUT THIS STATE PARK

The area is located 2 miles north and 3 miles east of Beaverville, in the extreme northeast corner of Iroquois County, about 80 miles south of Chicago. The majority of the area, 2,000 acres, is managed as a public hunting area. The remainder is a dedicated nature preserve. Nonconsumptive recreation, in the form of hiking and nature study, is available when the facility is closed to hunting.

Activities

❏ ATV/OHV	❏ Horseback Riding	❏ Fishing	❏ Wildlife
❏ Berry Picking	❏ Kayaking	❏ Hiking	❏ Bird Viewing
❏ Biking	❏ Photography	❏ Hunting	❏ Snowmobiling
❏ Boating	❏ Skiing	❏ Snowshoeing	❏ ....
❏ Canoeing	❏ Skijoring	❏ Swimming	❏ ....

Facilities

❏ ADA	❏ Visitor Center	❏ Museum	❏ ....
❏ Gift Shop	❏ Picnic Sites	❏ Restrooms	❏ ....

Notes

....
....
....
....

Passport Stamps

JAMES "PATE" PHILIP STATE PARK

DuPage, Kane

DATE(S) VISITED:...

☐ SPRING   ☐ SUMMER   ☐ FALL   ☐ WINTER

WEATHER			TEMP:		
☐	☐	☐	☐	☐	☐

ABOUT THIS STATE PARK

James "Pate" Philip State Park, originally known as Tri-County State Park, is an Illinois state park in DuPage County and Kane County. The park is named after James "Pate" Philip, a Republican politician.

Check In:.............................. Check Out:..............................

Lodging:.................................. Park hours:.......................

Who I Went With:..

Fee(s):.. Will I Return?   YES / NO

Rating ★ ★ ★ ★ ★

Activities

☐ ATV/OHV	☐ Horseback Riding	☐ Fishing	☐ Wildlife
☐ Berry Picking	☐ Kayaking	☐ Hiking	☐ Bird Viewing
☐ Biking	☐ Photography	☐ Hunting	☐ Snowmobiling
☐ Boating	☐ Skiing	☐ Snowshoeing	☐ ....
☐ Canoeing	☐ Skijoring	☐ Swimming	☐ ....

Facilities

☐ ADA	☐ Visitor Center	☐ Museum	☐ ....
☐ Gift Shop	☐ Picnic Sites	☐ Restrooms	☐ ....

Notes

....
....
....
....

Passport Stamps

JIM EDGAR PANTHER CREEK STATE FISH AND WILDLIFE AREA

DATE(S) VISITED:..

❏ SPRING   ❏ SUMMER   ❏ FALL   ❏ WINTER

WEATHER			TEMP:		
☀	🌤	☁	🌧	🌦	🌨
❏	❏	❏	❏	❏	❏

Check In:............................ Check Out:................................

Lodging:.................................. Park hours:........................

Who I Went With:..

Fee(s):... Will I Return? YES / NO

Rating ⭐ ⭐ ⭐ ⭐ ⭐

ABOUT THIS STATE PARK

The Jim Edgar Panther Creek State Fish and Wildlife Area (JEPC) is a conservation area located within Cass County. state of Illinois. It is 16,550 acres (6,698 ha) in size. A mix of plowed upland prairie and Panther Creek woodlands, the site is managed by the Illinois Department of Natural Resources. It is drained by the Sangamon River. It is named for former Governor of Illinois Jim Edgar.

Activities

❏ ATV/OHV   ❏ Horseback Riding   ❏ Fishing   ❏ Wildlife
❏ Berry Picking ❏ Kayaking   ❏ Hiking   ❏ Bird Viewing
❏ Biking   ❏ Photography   ❏ Hunting   ❏ Snowmobiling
❏ Boating   ❏ Skiing   ❏ Snowshoeing   ❏ ....
❏ Canoeing   ❏ Skijoring   ❏ Swimming   ❏ ....

Facilities

❏ ADA   ❏ Visitor Center   ❏ Museum   ❏ ....
❏ Gift Shop ❏ Picnic Sites   ❏ Restrooms   ❏ ....

Notes

....
....
....
....

Passport Stamps

JOHNSON-SAUK TRAIL STATE PARK Henry

DATE(S) VISITED:..

❑ SPRING ❑ SUMMER ❑ FALL ❑ WINTER

WEATHER	TEMP:

❑ ❑ ❑ ❑ ❑ ❑

ABOUT THIS STATE PARK

From cross-country skiing in the winter to a lazy picnic in the summer, from a fishing trip in the spring to exploring fields of wildflowers amidst the fall colors of the giant oaks, Johnson-Sauk Trail State Recreation Area truly is a park for all seasons. Located on a glacial moraine that forms the beautiful, rolling hills of Henry County in north-central Illinois, the park sits astride a trail that led Native Americans from Lake Michigan to the confluence of the Mississippi and Rock rivers.

Check In:.............................. Check Out:..............................

Lodging:.................................. Park hours:.......................

Who I Went With:..

Fee(s):.. Will I Return? YES / NO

Rating ⭐ ⭐ ⭐ ⭐ ⭐

Activities

❑ ATV/OHV
❑ Berry Picking
❑ Biking
❑ Boating
❑ Canoeing

❑ Horseback Riding
❑ Kayaking
❑ Photography
❑ Skiing
❑ Skijoring

❑ Fishing
❑ Hiking
❑ Hunting
❑ Snowshoeing
❑ Swimming

❑ Wildlife
❑ Bird Viewing
❑ Snowmobiling
❑ ....
❑ ....

Facilities

❑ ADA
❑ Gift Shop

❑ Visitor Center
❑ Picnic Sites

❑ Museum
❑ Restrooms

❑ ....
❑ ....

Notes

....
....
....
....

Passport Stamps

JUBILEE COLLEGE STATE PARK

Peoria

DATE(S) VISITED:..

❑ SPRING   ❑ SUMMER   ❑ FALL   ❑ WINTER

WEATHER	TEMP:
☀ ❑ 🌤❑ ☁❑ 🌧❑ 🌨❑ 🌦❑	

Check In:............................. Check Out:................................

Lodging:................................... Park hours:........................

Who I Went With:..

Fee(s):.. Will I Return?   YES / NO

Rating ⭐ ⭐ ⭐ ⭐ ⭐

ABOUT THIS STATE PARK

Jubilee College State Park is a 3,200-acre facility, located in Peoria County between the towns of Kickapoo and Brimfield, just off U.S. Route 150. This scenic area, with its rolling topography and meandering Jubilee Creek, offers a variety of outdoor recreation opportunities.

Activities

❑ ATV/OHV	❑ Horseback Riding	❑ Fishing	❑ Wildlife
❑ Berry Picking	❑ Kayaking	❑ Hiking	❑ Bird Viewing
❑ Biking	❑ Photography	❑ Hunting	❑ Snowmobiling
❑ Boating	❑ Skiing	❑ Snowshoeing	❑ ....
❑ Canoeing	❑ Skijoring	❑ Swimming	❑ ....

Facilities

❑ ADA	❑ Visitor Center	❑ Museum	❑ ....
❑ Gift Shop	❑ Picnic Sites	❑ Restrooms	❑ ....

Notes

....
....
....
....

Passport Stamps

KANKAKEE RIVER STATE PARK

Kankakee, Will

DATE(S) VISITED:...

❑ SPRING   ❑ SUMMER   ❑ FALL   ❑ WINTER

WEATHER	TEMP:
☀ ❄☁ ☁ ☁ ☁ ☁	
❑ ❑ ❑ ❑ ❑ ❑	

Check In:.............................. Check Out:..............................

Lodging:.................................. Park hours:........................

Who I Went With:..

Fee(s):.. Will I Return?   YES / NO

Rating ⭐ ⭐ ⭐ ⭐ ⭐

ABOUT THIS STATE PARK

The naturally channeled Kankakee River, listed on the Federal Clean Streams Register, is the focus of the park's popularity. Fishing the Kankakee River is great for landing smallmouth bass, channel catfish, walleye and Northern pike. Rock Creek also is a good angling spot. The park has boat ramps at the Warner Bridge Day Use Area and the Area 9 parking lot on the south side of the river.Seasonal hunting programs include archery deer, waterfowl, and upland game hunting.

Activities

❑ ATV/OHV	❑ Horseback Riding	❑ Fishing	❑ Wildlife
❑ Berry Picking	❑ Kayaking	❑ Hiking	❑ Bird Viewing
❑ Biking	❑ Photography	❑ Hunting	❑ Snowmobiling
❑ Boating	❑ Skiing	❑ Snowshoeing	❑ ....
❑ Canoeing	❑ Skijoring	❑ Swimming	❑ ....

Facilities

❑ ADA	❑ Visitor Center	❑ Museum	❑ ....
❑ Gift Shop	❑ Picnic Sites	❑ Restrooms	❑ ....

Notes

....
....
....
....

Passport Stamps

KASKASKIA RIVER STATE FISH & WILDLIFE AREA

St. Clair, Monroe, Randolph

DATE(S) VISITED:...

❑ SPRING   ❑ SUMMER   ❑ FALL   ❑ WINTER

WEATHER	TEMP:
☀ ❄☁ ☁ 🌧 ⛈ 🌨	
❑ ❑ ❑ ❑ ❑ ❑	

Check In:............................. Check Out:...............................

Lodging:................................. Park hours:........................

Who I Went With:...

Fee(s):.. Will I Return?   YES / NO

Rating   ⭐ ⭐ ⭐ ⭐ ⭐

ABOUT THIS STATE PARK

The Kaskaskia River State Fish & Wildlife Area is one of the largest state-owned and managed sites in Illinois. The area comprises more than 20,000 acres. Baldwin Lake, a 2,018-acre reservoir built by Illinois Power Company, is contained within Kaskaskia River SFWA. This lake serves as a source of cooling water a nearby electric generating station. Baldwin Lake is open to the public for fishing and is a major part of the area's waterfowl refuge.

Activities

❑ ATV/OHV	❑ Horseback Riding	❑ Fishing	❑ Wildlife
❑ Berry Picking	❑ Kayaking	❑ Hiking	❑ Bird Viewing
❑ Biking	❑ Photography	❑ Hunting	❑ Snowmobiling
❑ Boating	❑ Skiing	❑ Snowshoeing	❑ ....
❑ Canoeing	❑ Skijoring	❑ Swimming	❑ ....

Facilities

❑ ADA	❑ Visitor Center	❑ Museum	❑ ....
❑ Gift Shop	❑ Picnic Sites	❑ Restrooms	❑ ....

Notes

....
....
....
....

Passport Stamps

KICKAPOO STATE RECREATION AREA

Vermilion

DATE(S) VISITED:...

❑ SPRING   ❑ SUMMER   ❑ FALL   ❑ WINTER

WEATHER					TEMP:
☀ ❑	⛅ ❑	☁ ❑	🌧 ❑	🌦 ❑	🌨 ❑

Check In:............................. Check Out:...............................

Lodging:.................................... Park hours:........................

Who I Went With:...

Fee(s):.. Will I Return?   YES / NO

Rating ⭐ ⭐ ⭐ ⭐ ⭐

ABOUT THIS STATE PARK

Kickapoo State Park has 221 acres (89 ha) of ponds and lakes with nearly 35 miles (56 km) of hiking trails for many types of recreational activities including camping, canoeing, hunting, mountain biking, and fishing. In the winter season, ice fishing and cross-country skiing are popular pastimes for visitors to the park. There are 22 deep water ponds which are accessible to electric motor boats, canoes, and kayaks.

Activities

❑ ATV/OHV	❑ Horseback Riding	❑ Fishing	❑ Wildlife
❑ Berry Picking	❑ Kayaking	❑ Hiking	❑ Bird Viewing
❑ Biking	❑ Photography	❑ Hunting	❑ Snowmobiling
❑ Boating	❑ Skiing	❑ Snowshoeing	❑ ....
❑ Canoeing	❑ Skijoring	❑ Swimming	❑ ....

Facilities

❑ ADA	❑ Visitor Center	❑ Museum	❑ ....
❑ Gift Shop	❑ Picnic Sites	❑ Restrooms	❑ ....

Notes

....
....
....
....

Passport Stamps

KINKAID LAKE STATE FISH AND WILDLIFE AREA

Jackson

DATE(S) VISITED:...

❑ SPRING   ❑ SUMMER   ❑ FALL   ❑ WINTER

WEATHER			TEMP:		
☀	❄☁	☁	☁ⅷⅷ	☁💧	☁
❑	❑	❑	❑	❑	❑

Check In:.............................. Check Out:...............................

Lodging:.................................. Park hours:........................

Who I Went With:..

Fee(s):.. Will I Return?   YES / NO

Rating   ★ ★ ★ ★ ★

ABOUT THIS STATE PARK

Located in southwestern Illinois' Jackson County, Kinkaid Lake is approximately 5 miles north of Murphysboro and 100 miles southeast of St. Louis. Topography varies from sandstone bluff formations to rolling hills surrounding the lake where oaks and hickories predominate. Numerous flat contours are planted with prairie grasses, cool-season grasses and wildlife food plots.

Activities

❑ ATV/OHV	❑ Horseback Riding	❑ Fishing	❑ Wildlife
❑ Berry Picking	❑ Kayaking	❑ Hiking	❑ Bird Viewing
❑ Biking	❑ Photography	❑ Hunting	❑ Snowmobiling
❑ Boating	❑ Skiing	❑ Snowshoeing	❑ ....
❑ Canoeing	❑ Skijoring	❑ Swimming	❑ ....

Facilities

❑ ADA	❑ Visitor Center	❑ Museum	❑ ....
❑ Gift Shop	❑ Picnic Sites	❑ Restrooms	❑ ....

Notes

....
....
....
....

Passport Stamps

LAKE LE-AQUA-NA STATE PARK

Stephenson

DATE(S) VISITED:..

❑ SPRING ❑ SUMMER ❑ FALL ❑ WINTER

WEATHER	TEMP:
☀ ✶ ☁ ☁ ☁ ☁ ☁	
❑ ❑ ❑ ❑ ❑ ❑	

Check In:.............................. Check Out:..............................

Lodging:.................................. Park hours:.......................

Who I Went With:...

Fee(s):.. Will I Return? YES / NO

Rating ★ ★ ★ ★ ★

ABOUT THIS STATE PARK

Highlighted by a 40-acre lake and all the recreational opportunities there, the park also offers multi-use trails, picnic areas, and RV, tent, equestrian and youth group campgrounds. Lake Le-Aqua-Na's name is the result of a contest sponsored by the Stephenson County Sportsman's Club, one of the park's many sponsors. The name is a combination of the town of Lena and the Latin word for water, aqua.

Activities

❑ ATV/OHV	❑ Horseback Riding	❑ Fishing	❑ Wildlife
❑ Berry Picking	❑ Kayaking	❑ Hiking	❑ Bird Viewing
❑ Biking	❑ Photography	❑ Hunting	❑ Snowmobiling
❑ Boating	❑ Skiing	❑ Snowshoeing	❑ ....
❑ Canoeing	❑ Skijoring	❑ Swimming	❑ ....

Facilities

❑ ADA	❑ Visitor Center	❑ Museum	❑ ....
❑ Gift Shop	❑ Picnic Sites	❑ Restrooms	❑ ....

Notes

....
....
....
....

Passport Stamps

LAKE MURPHYSBORO STATE PARK

Jackson

DATE(S) VISITED:..

☐ SPRING   ☐ SUMMER   ☐ FALL   ☐ WINTER

WEATHER			TEMP:		
☀	❄☁	☁	☁🌧	☁🌨	☁
☐	☐	☐	☐	☐	☐

Check In:................................ Check Out:................................

Lodging:.................................. Park hours:........................

Who I Went With:..

Fee(s):.. Will I Return?   YES / NO

Rating ★ ★ ★ ★ ★

ABOUT THIS STATE PARK

Beautiful rolling hills and woods surround star-shaped Lake Murphysboro and provide a wonderful backdrop for boating, fishing, picnicking, camping and hiking. Located in Jackson County about 1 mile west of Murphysboro off Route 149, the 1,022-acre state park is the perfect place to enjoy the great outdoors.

Activities

☐ ATV/OHV   ☐ Horseback Riding   ☐ Fishing   ☐ Wildlife

☐ Berry Picking   ☐ Kayaking   ☐ Hiking   ☐ Bird Viewing

☐ Biking   ☐ Photography   ☐ Hunting   ☐ Snowmobiling

☐ Boating   ☐ Skiing   ☐ Snowshoeing   ☐ ....

☐ Canoeing   ☐ Skijoring   ☐ Swimming   ☐ ....

Facilities

☐ ADA   ☐ Visitor Center   ☐ Museum   ☐ ....

☐ Gift Shop   ☐ Picnic Sites   ☐ Restrooms   ☐ ....

Notes

....

....

....

....

Passport Stamps

LASALLE LAKE STATE FISH & WILDLIFE AREA — LaSalle

DATE(S) VISITED:...

❑ SPRING   ❑ SUMMER   ❑ FALL   ❑ WINTER

WEATHER	TEMP:
☀ 🌤 ☁ 🌧 🌦 🌨	
❑ ❑ ❑ ❑ ❑ ❑	

Check In:............................ Check Out:............................

Lodging:................................. Park hours:.....................

Who I Went With:..

Fee(s):.. Will I Return?   YES / NO

Rating
⭐ ⭐ ⭐ ⭐ ⭐

ABOUT THIS STATE PARK

LaSalle Lake, a manmade, 2,058-acre lake 8 miles southeast of Marseilles, is popular among anglers. Serving as a cooling lake for Commonwealth Edison's LaSalle Power Station, the lake is formed by levees that rise above the surrounding land. While this perched construction helps the lake catch the wind to cool the impounded water, it can result in extremely hazardous conditions for unwary boaters.

Activities

❑ ATV/OHV	❑ Horseback Riding	❑ Fishing	❑ Wildlife
❑ Berry Picking	❑ Kayaking	❑ Hiking	❑ Bird Viewing
❑ Biking	❑ Photography	❑ Hunting	❑ Snowmobiling
❑ Boating	❑ Skiing	❑ Snowshoeing	❑ ....
❑ Canoeing	❑ Skijoring	❑ Swimming	❑ ....

Facilities

❑ ADA	❑ Visitor Center	❑ Museum	❑ ....
❑ Gift Shop	❑ Picnic Sites	❑ Restrooms	❑ ....

Notes
....
....
....
....

Passport Stamps

LINCOLN TRAIL HOMESTEAD STATE MEMORIAL

Macon

DATE(S) VISITED:...

❑ SPRING ❑ SUMMER ❑ FALL ❑ WINTER

WEATHER	TEMP:

❑ ❑ ❑ ❑ ❑ ❑

Check In:............................. Check Out:..............................

Lodging:.................................. Park hours:........................

Who I Went With:..

Fee(s):.. Will I Return? YES / NO

Rating ⭐ ⭐ ⭐ ⭐ ⭐

ABOUT THIS STATE PARK

The Lincoln Trail Homestead State Park and Memorial is a 162 acre (0.65 km²) state park located on the Sangamon River in Macon County near Harristown, Illinois. This important historic site, only 12 miles Southwest of Decatur, offers hiking, canoeing, picnicking, recreational activities, and a glimpse into the past. The park offers a unique view of central Illinois.

Activities

❑ ATV/OHV	❑ Horseback Riding	❑ Fishing	❑ Wildlife
❑ Berry Picking	❑ Kayaking	❑ Hiking	❑ Bird Viewing
❑ Biking	❑ Photography	❑ Hunting	❑ Snowmobiling
❑ Boating	❑ Skiing	❑ Snowshoeing	❑ ....
❑ Canoeing	❑ Skijoring	❑ Swimming	❑ ....

Facilities

❑ ADA	❑ Visitor Center	❑ Museum	❑ ....
❑ Gift Shop	❑ Picnic Sites	❑ Restrooms	❑ ....

Notes

....
....
....
....

Passport Stamps

LINCOLN TRAIL STATE PARK

Clark

DATE(S) VISITED:..

❏ SPRING ❏ SUMMER ❏ FALL ❏ WINTER

WEATHER					TEMP:
❏	❏	❏	❏	❏	❏

Check In:............................... Check Out:..............................

Lodging:................................ Park hours:........................

Who I Went With:..

Fee(s):............................... Will I Return? YES / NO

Rating ⭐ ⭐ ⭐ ⭐ ⭐

ABOUT THIS STATE PARK

Visitors to the 1,023-acre park can enjoy the sights of an American Beech woods; wildflowers, including the unusual squaw-root and beech drops; and recreational activities such as boating, camping, fishing, hiking and winter sports. There is truly something for everyone.

Activities

❏ ATV/OHV   ❏ Horseback Riding   ❏ Fishing   ❏ Wildlife
❏ Berry Picking   ❏ Kayaking   ❏ Hiking   ❏ Bird Viewing
❏ Biking   ❏ Photography   ❏ Hunting   ❏ Snowmobiling
❏ Boating   ❏ Skiing   ❏ Snowshoeing   ❏ ....
❏ Canoeing   ❏ Skijoring   ❏ Swimming   ❏ ....

Facilities

❏ ADA   ❏ Visitor Center   ❏ Museum   ❏ ....
❏ Gift Shop   ❏ Picnic Sites   ❏ Restrooms   ❏ ....

Notes
....
....
....
....

Passport Stamps

LOWDEN STATE PARK

Ogle

DATE(S) VISITED:..

❏ SPRING   ❏ SUMMER   ❏ FALL   ❏ WINTER

| WEATHER | TEMP: |

☀ ❏   ✴☁ ❏   ☁ ❏   ☁☷ ❏   ☁💧 ❏   ☁ ❏

Check In:.............................. Check Out:..............................

Lodging:................................. Park hours:.......................

Who I Went With:..

Fee(s):.. Will I Return?   YES / NO

Rating   ★ ★ ★ ★ ★

ABOUT THIS STATE PARK

One of the most picturesque sites along the Rock River is just north of Oregon in Ogle County. Legend has it that Chief Black Hawk, as he left the area after the Black Hawk War, talked of the beauty of the area and admonished his captors to care for the land as he and his people had. Lowden State Park was established to care for the land and allow visitors to share in the beauty as well. The park serves as a memorial to Gov. Frank O. Lowden, who served Illinois during World War I.

Activities

❏ ATV/OHV	❏ Horseback Riding	❏ Fishing	❏ Wildlife
❏ Berry Picking	❏ Kayaking	❏ Hiking	❏ Bird Viewing
❏ Biking	❏ Photography	❏ Hunting	❏ Snowmobiling
❏ Boating	❏ Skiing	❏ Snowshoeing	❏ ....
❏ Canoeing	❏ Skijoring	❏ Swimming	❏ ....

Facilities

❏ ADA	❏ Visitor Center	❏ Museum	❏ ....
❏ Gift Shop	❏ Picnic Sites	❏ Restrooms	❏ ....

Notes

....
....
....
....

Passport Stamps

MACKINAW RIVER STATE FISH AND WILDLIFE AREA

Tazewell

DATE(S) VISITED:..

❑ SPRING ❑ SUMMER ❑ FALL ❑ WINTER

ABOUT THIS STATE PARK

Bisected by the picturesque river whose name it bears, Mackinaw River State Fish & Wildlife Area provides hunting, fishing, canoeing and an opportunity to interact with nature. The diverse, minimally developed area, consisting of rolling timbered hills and former farmland, is 18 miles west of Bloomington Normal and 3 miles northeast of the town of Mackinaw, between Interstate 74 and Illinois Route 9.

WEATHER						TEMP:
❑	❑	❑	❑	❑	❑	

Check In:............................ Check Out:............................

Lodging:.................................. Park hours:.......................

Who I Went With:..

Fee(s):.. Will I Return? YES / NO

Rating ★ ★ ★ ★ ★

Activities

❑ ATV/OHV   ❑ Horseback Riding   ❑ Fishing   ❑ Wildlife
❑ Berry Picking   ❑ Kayaking   ❑ Hiking   ❑ Bird Viewing
❑ Biking   ❑ Photography   ❑ Hunting   ❑ Snowmobiling
❑ Boating   ❑ Skiing   ❑ Snowshoeing   ❑ ....
❑ Canoeing   ❑ Skijoring   ❑ Swimming   ❑ ....

Facilities

❑ ADA   ❑ Visitor Center   ❑ Museum   ❑ ....
❑ Gift Shop   ❑ Picnic Sites   ❑ Restrooms   ❑ ....

Notes

....
....
....
....

Passport Stamps

MARSHALL STATE FISH & WILDLIFE AREA

Marshall

DATE(S) VISITED:..

❑ SPRING ❑ SUMMER ❑ FALL ❑ WINTER

WEATHER			TEMP:		
☀	❄☁	☁	☁⫯⫯	☁⫰	☁⫯
❑	❑	❑	❑	❑	❑

Check In:............................ Check Out:............................

Lodging:............................. Park hours:........................

Who I Went With:..

Fee(s):... Will I Return? YES / NO

Rating ★ ★ ★ ★ ★

ABOUT THIS STATE PARK

The Spring Beach Unit contains 1,642 acres (537 acres of water) on the west side of the Illinois River between Sparland and Chillicothe. The unit spans Marshall and Peoria counties. There is a 6-acre picnic area, fishing, and access to hunting and hiking trails adjacent to Route 29. The habitat ranges from upland forest to riverbottom to cropland.

Activities

❑ ATV/OHV	❑ Horseback Riding	❑ Fishing	❑ Wildlife
❑ Berry Picking	❑ Kayaking	❑ Hiking	❑ Bird Viewing
❑ Biking	❑ Photography	❑ Hunting	❑ Snowmobiling
❑ Boating	❑ Skiing	❑ Snowshoeing	❑ ....
❑ Canoeing	❑ Skijoring	❑ Swimming	❑ ....

Facilities

❑ ADA	❑ Visitor Center	❑ Museum	❑ ....
❑ Gift Shop	❑ Picnic Sites	❑ Restrooms	❑ ....

Notes

....
....
....
....

Passport Stamps

MATTHIESSEN STATE PARK | LaSalle

DATE(S) VISITED:..

☐ SPRING ☐ SUMMER ☐ FALL ☐ WINTER

| WEATHER | TEMP: |

☐ ☐ ☐ ☐ ☐ ☐

Check In:............................ Check Out:..............................

Lodging:................................. Park hours:........................

Who I Went With:...

Fee(s):.. Will I Return? YES / NO

Rating ⭐ ⭐ ⭐ ⭐ ⭐

ABOUT THIS STATE PARK

Canyons, streams, prairie and forest combine to delight visitors at Matthiessen State Park. Located in LaSalle County, approximately 4 miles south of Utica, and 3 miles east of Oglesby, Matthiessen is a paradise for those interested in geology, as well as recreation. Visitors can expect to see beautiful rock formations in addition to unusual and abundant vegetation and wildlife. All of this, along with park and picnic facilities, make Matthiessen State Park a popular choice for an outing.

Activities

☐ ATV/OHV
☐ Berry Picking
☐ Biking
☐ Boating
☐ Canoeing

☐ Horseback Riding
☐ Kayaking
☐ Photography
☐ Skiing
☐ Skijoring

☐ Fishing
☐ Hiking
☐ Hunting
☐ Snowshoeing
☐ Swimming

☐ Wildlife
☐ Bird Viewing
☐ Snowmobiling
☐ ....
☐ ....

Facilities

☐ ADA
☐ Gift Shop

☐ Visitor Center
☐ Picnic Sites

☐ Museum
☐ Restrooms

☐ ....
☐ ....

Notes

....
....
....
....

Passport Stamps

MAUTINO STATE FISH AND WILDLIFE AREA

Bureau

DATE(S) VISITED:...

❑ SPRING ❑ SUMMER ❑ FALL ❑ WINTER

WEATHER	TEMP:

❑ ❑ ❑ ❑ ❑ ❑

Check In:............................. Check Out:.............................

Lodging:................................. Park hours:.............................

Who I Went With:..

Fee(s):... Will I Return? YES / NO

Rating ⭐ ⭐ ⭐ ⭐ ⭐

ABOUT THIS STATE PARK

Mautino State Fish and Wildlife Area is a former strip mine site of 900 acres that is now home to a total of 16 ponds and lakes, making it an idyllic location for kayaking, canoeing, and boating. Located south of Sheffield and west of Buda in Bureau County, the site is named for former State Representative Richard "Dick" Mautino, who served in the Illinois General Assembly from 1975 until his death in 1991.

Activities

❑ ATV/OHV	❑ Horseback Riding	❑ Fishing	❑ Wildlife
❑ Berry Picking	❑ Kayaking	❑ Hiking	❑ Bird Viewing
❑ Biking	❑ Photography	❑ Hunting	❑ Snowmobiling
❑ Boating	❑ Skiing	❑ Snowshoeing	❑ ....
❑ Canoeing	❑ Skijoring	❑ Swimming	❑ ....

Facilities

❑ ADA	❑ Visitor Center	❑ Museum	❑ ....
❑ Gift Shop	❑ Picnic Sites	❑ Restrooms	❑ ....

Notes

....
....
....
....

Passport Stamps

MAZONIA/BRAIDWOOD STATE FISH AND WILDLIFE AREA

Grundy

DATE(S) VISITED:...

☐ SPRING ☐ SUMMER ☐ FALL ☐ WINTER

WEATHER	TEMP:

☐ ☐ ☐ ☐ ☐ ☐

ABOUT THIS STATE PARK

The IDNR Mazonia-Braidwood complex is one of northeast Illinois' most popular destinations for hunting and fishing. Mazonia State Fish and Wildlife Area features 1,017 acres and is located in Grundy County 3 miles southeast of Braidwood on Illinois Route 53 and Huston Road. Braidwood Lake Fish and Wildlife Area - including the partially perched cooling lake for the Braidwood Generating Station - is 2,640 acres.

Check In:............................. Check Out:...............................

Lodging:.................................. Park hours:........................

Who I Went With:..

Fee(s):... Will I Return? YES / NO

Rating ⭐ ⭐ ⭐ ⭐ ⭐

Activities

☐ ATV/OHV
☐ Berry Picking
☐ Biking
☐ Boating
☐ Canoeing

☐ Horseback Riding
☐ Kayaking
☐ Photography
☐ Skiing
☐ Skijoring

☐ Fishing
☐ Hiking
☐ Hunting
☐ Snowshoeing
☐ Swimming

☐ Wildlife
☐ Bird Viewing
☐ Snowmobiling
☐ ....
☐ ....

Facilities

☐ ADA
☐ Gift Shop

☐ Visitor Center
☐ Picnic Sites

☐ Museum
☐ Restrooms

☐ ....
☐ ....

Notes

....
....
....
....

Passport Stamps

DATE(S) VISITED:...

❑ SPRING   ❑ SUMMER   ❑ FALL   ❑ WINTER

WEATHER			TEMP:		
❑	❑	❑	❑	❑	❑

ABOUT THIS STATE PARK

Mermet Lake State Fish and Wildlife Area is an old cypress southern Illinois swamp managed as one of the state's most outstanding waterfowl hunting locales. While Mermet Lake was developed primarily for duck hunting, Canada, blue and snow geese frequent the area each winter. While Mermet Lake is a popular hunting and fishing destination, there are also hiking trails and picnic tables for site visitors. Mermet Lake is also home to the Illinois Pro/Am National Archery Tournament in late June.

Check In:............................. Check Out:...............................

Lodging:................................... Park hours:........................

Who I Went With:..

Fee(s):... Will I Return?   YES / NO

Rating ⭐ ⭐ ⭐ ⭐ ⭐

Activities

❑ ATV/OHV	❑ Horseback Riding	❑ Fishing	❑ Wildlife
❑ Berry Picking	❑ Kayaking	❑ Hiking	❑ Bird Viewing
❑ Biking	❑ Photography	❑ Hunting	❑ Snowmobiling
❑ Boating	❑ Skiing	❑ Snowshoeing	❑ ....
❑ Canoeing	❑ Skijoring	❑ Swimming	❑ ....

Facilities

❑ ADA	❑ Visitor Center	❑ Museum	❑ ....
❑ Gift Shop	❑ Picnic Sites	❑ Restrooms	❑ ....

Notes

....
....
....
....

Passport Stamps

MIDDLE FORK STATE FISH AND WILDLIFE AREA

Vermilion

DATE(S) VISITED:..

❑ SPRING ❑ SUMMER ❑ FALL ❑ WINTER

WEATHER	TEMP:

❑ ❑ ❑ ❑ ❑ ❑

ABOUT THIS STATE PARK

The Middle Fork State Fish and Wildlife Area is located 6 miles north of the Interstate 74 exit at Oakwood. The area consists of 2,700 acres of grass, forest and cropland, and provides excellent wildlife habitat. The site received its name from the Middle Fork branch of the Vermilion River which flows between Kennekuk Cove County Park and Middle Fork State Fish & Wildlife Area. At Kickapoo you can enjoy family camping, picnicking, fishing, boating, mountain biking and rent a horse for a short trail ride.

Check In:............................. Check Out:.............................

Lodging:................................. Park hours:.......................

Who I Went With:..

Fee(s):.. Will I Return? YES / NO

Rating ⭐ ⭐ ⭐ ⭐ ⭐

Activities

❑ ATV/OHV ❑ Horseback Riding ❑ Fishing ❑ Wildlife
❑ Berry Picking ❑ Kayaking ❑ Hiking ❑ Bird Viewing
❑ Biking ❑ Photography ❑ Hunting ❑ Snowmobiling
❑ Boating ❑ Skiing ❑ Snowshoeing ❑ ....
❑ Canoeing ❑ Skijoring ❑ Swimming ❑ ....

Facilities

❑ ADA ❑ Visitor Center ❑ Museum ❑ ....
❑ Gift Shop ❑ Picnic Sites ❑ Restrooms ❑ ....

Notes

....
....
....
....

Passport Stamps

MISSISSIPPI PALISADES STATE PARK   Carroll

DATE(S) VISITED:..

❑ SPRING   ❑ SUMMER   ❑ FALL   ❑ WINTER

WEATHER	TEMP:
☀ ❇ ☁ 🌧 ⛈ 🌨	
❑ ❑ ❑ ❑ ❑ ❑	

Check In:............................. Check Out:...............................

Lodging:.................................. Park hours:........................

Who I Went With:..

Fee(s):... Will I Return?   YES / NO

Rating ★ ★ ★ ★ ★

ABOUT THIS STATE PARK

The Native American pathfinders along the rock palisades of the Mississippi River did as present-day hikers do -- in coursing the bluffs, they took the paths of least resistance. The trails at the Mississippi Palisades, especially the park's southern routes, put you in touch with the past. Located near the confluence of the Mississippi and Apple rivers in northwestern Illinois, the 2,500-acre Mississippi Palisades State Park is rich in Native American history.

Activities

❑ ATV/OHV	❑ Horseback Riding	❑ Fishing	❑ Wildlife
❑ Berry Picking	❑ Kayaking	❑ Hiking	❑ Bird Viewing
❑ Biking	❑ Photography	❑ Hunting	❑ Snowmobiling
❑ Boating	❑ Skiing	❑ Snowshoeing	❑ ....
❑ Canoeing	❑ Skijoring	❑ Swimming	❑ ....

Facilities

❑ ADA	❑ Visitor Center	❑ Museum	❑ ....
❑ Gift Shop	❑ Picnic Sites	❑ Restrooms	❑ ....

Notes

....
....
....
....

Passport Stamps

MISSISSIPPI RIVER STATE FISH AND WILDLIFE AREA

Jersey, Calhoun

DATE(S) VISITED:...

❑ SPRING   ❑ SUMMER   ❑ FALL   ❑ WINTER

WEATHER	TEMP:
☀ ❑ 🌨 ❑ ☁ ❑ 🌧 ❑ 🌨 ❑ 🌨 ❑	

Check In:............................. Check Out:..............................

Lodging:.................................. Park hours:.......................

Who I Went With:...

Fee(s):.. Will I Return? YES / NO

Rating ⭐ ⭐ ⭐ ⭐ ⭐

ABOUT THIS STATE PARK

Imagine an area that includes 15 wildlife management areas and 13 public access areas spanning more than 24,000 acres and scattered along 75 miles of two major rivers. Add to this awe-inspiring bluffs that tower over the river valley, providing breathtaking views, and you begin to get some idea of what awaits you at the Mississippi River State Fish and Wildlife Area.

Activities

❑ ATV/OHV	❑ Horseback Riding	❑ Fishing	❑ Wildlife
❑ Berry Picking	❑ Kayaking	❑ Hiking	❑ Bird Viewing
❑ Biking	❑ Photography	❑ Hunting	❑ Snowmobiling
❑ Boating	❑ Skiing	❑ Snowshoeing	❑ ....
❑ Canoeing	❑ Skijoring	❑ Swimming	❑ ....

Facilities

❑ ADA	❑ Visitor Center	❑ Museum	❑ ....
❑ Gift Shop	❑ Picnic Sites	❑ Restrooms	❑ ....

Notes

....
....
....
....

Passport Stamps

MORAINE HILLS STATE PARK

McHenry

DATE(S) VISITED:..

❑ SPRING   ❑ SUMMER   ❑ FALL   ❑ WINTER

WEATHER	TEMP:

❑ ❑ ❑ ❑ ❑ ❑

ABOUT THIS STATE PARK

Moraine Hills State Park is a recreational paradise in northeast Illinois. The state park's 2,200 acres is composed of wetlands and lakes. The diverse habitats support an abundance of plants and a great variety of wildlife to enjoy along ten-plus miles of trails. McHenry Dam State Park is located along the east side of the Fox River and overlooks McHenry Lock & Dam. The river attracts anglers, waterfowl, eagles, birders and photographers alike.

Check In:.............................. Check Out:..............................

Lodging:................................. Park hours:........................

Who I Went With:...

Fee(s):.. Will I Return?   YES / NO

Rating ⭐⭐⭐⭐⭐

Activities

❑ ATV/OHV
❑ Berry Picking
❑ Biking
❑ Boating
❑ Canoeing

❑ Horseback Riding
❑ Kayaking
❑ Photography
❑ Skiing
❑ Skijoring

❑ Fishing
❑ Hiking
❑ Hunting
❑ Snowshoeing
❑ Swimming

❑ Wildlife
❑ Bird Viewing
❑ Snowmobiling
❑ ....
❑ ....

Facilities

❑ ADA
❑ Gift Shop

❑ Visitor Center
❑ Picnic Sites

❑ Museum
❑ Restrooms

❑ ....
❑ ....

Notes

....
....
....
....

Passport Stamps

MORAINE VIEW STATE RECREATION AREA   McLean

DATE(S) VISITED:...

☐ SPRING   ☐ SUMMER   ☐ FALL   ☐ WINTER

ABOUT THIS STATE PARK

WEATHER		TEMP:

☐ ☐ ☐ ☐ ☐ ☐

With fully developed facilities for picnicking, camping, hiking, swimming, fishing, boating, horseback riding and hunting, the 1,687-acre Moraine View State Recreation Area, with its 158-acre lake, is a beautiful, convenient and accessible locale for relaxation and recreation.

Check In:.............................. Check Out:...............................

Lodging:................................ Park hours:........................

Who I Went With:...

Fee(s):.. Will I Return?   YES / NO

Rating   ★ ★ ★ ★ ★

Activities

☐ ATV/OHV   ☐ Horseback Riding   ☐ Fishing   ☐ Wildlife
☐ Berry Picking   ☐ Kayaking   ☐ Hiking   ☐ Bird Viewing
☐ Biking   ☐ Photography   ☐ Hunting   ☐ Snowmobiling
☐ Boating   ☐ Skiing   ☐ Snowshoeing   ☐ ....
☐ Canoeing   ☐ Skijoring   ☐ Swimming   ☐ ....

Facilities

☐ ADA   ☐ Visitor Center   ☐ Museum   ☐ ....
☐ Gift Shop   ☐ Picnic Sites   ☐ Restrooms   ☐ ....

Notes

....
....
....
....

Passport Stamps

DATE(S) VISITED:..

☐ SPRING   ☐ SUMMER   ☐ FALL   ☐ WINTER

WEATHER						TEMP:
☐	☐	☐	☐	☐	☐	

Check In:............................ Check Out:...............................

Lodging:.................................. Park hours:.........................

Who I Went With:...

Fee(s):.. Will I Return? YES / NO

Rating ★ ★ ★ ★ ★

ABOUT THIS STATE PARK

A trip to picturesque Morrison-Rockwood State Park offers many memorable experiences. A large sign in the shape of Illinois, fashioned from angle iron by a blacksmith, greets visitors at the entrance. Beautiful Lake Carlton, a stream-fed reservoir, features an abundance of ducks and geese and is considered a prime location for fishing. Morrison-Rockwood is a popular spot for a family outing at the Lakeview picnic area, or watching birds among the hickory, ash, oak and walnut trees.

Activities

☐ ATV/OHV	☐ Horseback Riding	☐ Fishing	☐ Wildlife
☐ Berry Picking	☐ Kayaking	☐ Hiking	☐ Bird Viewing
☐ Biking	☐ Photography	☐ Hunting	☐ Snowmobiling
☐ Boating	☐ Skiing	☐ Snowshoeing	☐ ....
☐ Canoeing	☐ Skijoring	☐ Swimming	☐ ....

Facilities

☐ ADA	☐ Visitor Center	☐ Museum	☐ ....
☐ Gift Shop	☐ Picnic Sites	☐ Restrooms	☐ ....

Notes

....
....
....
....

Passport Stamps

NAUVOO STATE PARK

Hancock

DATE(S) VISITED:...

❑ SPRING   ❑ SUMMER   ❑ FALL   ❑ WINTER

ABOUT THIS STATE PARK

Nauvoo's first name was Quashquema, a Fox Indian word meaning "peaceful place." Nauvoo, a Hebrew word for "beautiful place" or "pleasant land", is a historic town and the backdrop for Nauvoo State Park. The 148-acre park, on the south edge of Nauvoo along Illinois Route 96, includes a 13-acre lake with a mile-long shoreline. In addition to fishing, boating, camping and hiking, people return to these serene surroundings for the park's recreational features, its annual grape festival and to soak up the area's history.

WEATHER	TEMP:

☀ ❑   ❄☁ ❑   ☁ ❑   🌧 ❑   🌨 ❑   ❄ ❑

Check In:.............................. Check Out:...............................

Lodging:.................................. Park hours:.......................

Who I Went With:...

Fee(s):.. Will I Return?   YES / NO

Rating   ★ ★ ★ ★ ★

Activities

❑ ATV/OHV   ❑ Horseback Riding   ❑ Fishing   ❑ Wildlife
❑ Berry Picking ❑ Kayaking   ❑ Hiking   ❑ Bird Viewing
❑ Biking   ❑ Photography   ❑ Hunting   ❑ Snowmobiling
❑ Boating   ❑ Skiing   ❑ Snowshoeing   ❑ ....
❑ Canoeing   ❑ Skijoring   ❑ Swimming   ❑ ....

Facilities

❑ ADA   ❑ Visitor Center   ❑ Museum   ❑ ....
❑ Gift Shop   ❑ Picnic Sites   ❑ Restrooms   ❑ ....

Notes

....
....
....
....

Passport Stamps

NEWTON LAKE STATE FISH AND WILDLIFE AREA

Jasper

DATE(S) VISITED:..

❑ SPRING   ❑ SUMMER   ❑ FALL   ❑ WINTER

WEATHER	TEMP:

ABOUT THIS STATE PARK

In 1979, the Illinois Department of Natural Resources signed a lease with Central Illinois Public Service Company which designated the 1,775-acre Newton Lake and 540 acres of shoreline as a day use conservation area. By agreement, recreational activities at Newton Lake State Fish and Wildlife Area consist of fishing, picnicking, trail use and deer hunting.

Check In:.............................. Check Out:...............................

Lodging:.................................. Park hours:........................

Who I Went With:...

Fee(s):... Will I Return?   YES / NO

Rating ★ ★ ★ ★ ★

Activities

❑ ATV/OHV   ❑ Horseback Riding   ❑ Fishing   ❑ Wildlife
❑ Berry Picking   ❑ Kayaking   ❑ Hiking   ❑ Bird Viewing
❑ Biking   ❑ Photography   ❑ Hunting   ❑ Snowmobiling
❑ Boating   ❑ Skiing   ❑ Snowshoeing   ❑ ....
❑ Canoeing   ❑ Skijoring   ❑ Swimming   ❑ ....

Facilities

❑ ADA   ❑ Visitor Center   ❑ Museum   ❑ ....
❑ Gift Shop   ❑ Picnic Sites   ❑ Restrooms   ❑ ....

Notes

....
....
....
....

Passport Stamps

NORTH POINT MARINA

Lake

DATE(S) VISITED:..

❏ SPRING ❏ SUMMER ❏ FALL ❏ WINTER

WEATHER						TEMP:
❏	❏	❏	❏	❏	❏	

Check In:............................. Check Out:...............................

Lodging:.................................. Park hours:........................

Who I Went With:..

Fee(s):... Will I Return? YES / NO

Rating ⭐ ⭐ ⭐ ⭐ ⭐

ABOUT THIS STATE PARK

The largest marina on the Great Lakes - a world-class facility offering public access to Lake Michigan from a quiet, serene and safe setting on the breathtakingly beautiful Illinois lakeshore. North Point Marina is adjacent to Illinois Beach State Park, one of the nation's most beautiful state parks, preserving the last remaining shore in the state with natural coastal dunes and wetlands, high quality coastal fauna, outstanding recreation, and the popular Illinois Beach Resort and Conference Center.

Activities

❏ ATV/OHV	❏ Horseback Riding	❏ Fishing	❏ Wildlife
❏ Berry Picking	❏ Kayaking	❏ Hiking	❏ Bird Viewing
❏ Biking	❏ Photography	❏ Hunting	❏ Snowmobiling
❏ Boating	❏ Skiing	❏ Snowshoeing	❏ ....
❏ Canoeing	❏ Skijoring	❏ Swimming	❏ ....

Facilities

❏ ADA	❏ Visitor Center	❏ Museum	❏ ....
❏ Gift Shop	❏ Picnic Sites	❏ Restrooms	❏ ....

Notes

....
....
....
....

Passport Stamps

DATE(S) VISITED:...

❑ SPRING   ❑ SUMMER   ❑ FALL   ❑ WINTER

WEATHER			TEMP:		
☀	❄☁	☁	🌧	🌧	🌧
❑	❑	❑	❑	❑	❑

Check In:............................. Check Out:...........................

Lodging:................................ Park hours:.......................

Who I Went With:...

Fee(s):... Will I Return? YES / NO

Rating ⭐⭐⭐⭐⭐

ABOUT THIS STATE PARK

Total area: 1,181 acres. Huntable acres: 305. This area is a bottomland of sloughs, lakes, and low timbered ridges. Practically all of the area is subject to and conditioned by periodic flooding of the Illinois River. As time and budget allow, this area is targeted for restoration activities and enhancement of wildlife habitat.

Activities

❑ ATV/OHV	❑ Horseback Riding	❑ Fishing	❑ Wildlife
❑ Berry Picking	❑ Kayaking	❑ Hiking	❑ Bird Viewing
❑ Biking	❑ Photography	❑ Hunting	❑ Snowmobiling
❑ Boating	❑ Skiing	❑ Snowshoeing	❑ ....
❑ Canoeing	❑ Skijoring	❑ Swimming	❑ ....

Facilities

❑ ADA	❑ Visitor Center	❑ Museum	❑ ....
❑ Gift Shop	❑ Picnic Sites	❑ Restrooms	❑ ....

Notes

....
....
....
....

Passport Stamps

PERE MARQUETTE STATE PARK

Jersey

DATE(S) VISITED:..

☐ SPRING   ☐ SUMMER   ☐ FALL   ☐ WINTER

WEATHER					
☀	☁	☁	☔	☁	☁
☐	☐	☐	☐	☐	☐

TEMP:

Check In:............................. Check Out:.............................

Lodging:................................. Park hours:.......................

Who I Went With:..

Fee(s):.. Will I Return? YES / NO

Rating
⭐ ⭐ ⭐ ⭐ ⭐

ABOUT THIS STATE PARK

Pere Marquette State Park is a nature lover's paradise. In addition to enjoying the spectacular views of the Illinois River and its backwaters from several points atop the bluffs, visitors can take advantage of a variety of year-round recreational opportunities, including horseback riding, camping, hiking, fishing, hunting and boating.

Activities

☐ ATV/OHV	☐ Horseback Riding	☐ Fishing	☐ Wildlife
☐ Berry Picking	☐ Kayaking	☐ Hiking	☐ Bird Viewing
☐ Biking	☐ Photography	☐ Hunting	☐ Snowmobiling
☐ Boating	☐ Skiing	☐ Snowshoeing	☐ ....
☐ Canoeing	☐ Skijoring	☐ Swimming	☐ ....

Facilities

☐ ADA	☐ Visitor Center	☐ Museum	☐ ....
☐ Gift Shop	☐ Picnic Sites	☐ Restrooms	☐ ....

Notes
....
....
....
....

Passport Stamps

PINEY CREEK RAVINE STATE NATURAL AREA

Jackson, Randolph

DATE(S) VISITED:..

❑ SPRING   ❑ SUMMER   ❑ FALL   ❑ WINTER

WEATHER			TEMP:		
☀	☁	☁	☁	☁	☁
❑	❑	❑	❑	❑	❑

Check In:............................. Check Out:.............................

Lodging:.................................. Park hours:........................

Who I Went With:...

Fee(s):... Will I Return?   YES / NO

Rating ★ ★ ★ ★ ★

ABOUT THIS STATE PARK

West of DuQuoin and south of Steeleville on the Randolph-Jackson County line is a unique 198-acre area known as Piney Creek Ravine State Natural Area. Purchased in 1972 for its rare plant species and other natural features, it is one of only two locations in the state where short-leaf pines grow naturally. Piney Creek Ravine is dedicated nature preserve within the Illinois State Nature Preserve system.

Activities

❑ ATV/OHV	❑ Horseback Riding	❑ Fishing	❑ Wildlife
❑ Berry Picking	❑ Kayaking	❑ Hiking	❑ Bird Viewing
❑ Biking	❑ Photography	❑ Hunting	❑ Snowmobiling
❑ Boating	❑ Skiing	❑ Snowshoeing	❑ ....
❑ Canoeing	❑ Skijoring	❑ Swimming	❑ ....

Facilities

❑ ADA	❑ Visitor Center	❑ Museum	❑ ....
❑ Gift Shop	❑ Picnic Sites	❑ Restrooms	❑ ....

Notes

....

....

....

....

Passport Stamps

POWERTON LAKE STATE FISH AND WILDLIFE AREA

Jackson, Randolph

DATE(S) VISITED:..

❑ SPRING ❑ SUMMER ❑ FALL ❑ WINTER

ABOUT THIS STATE PARK

WEATHER			TEMP:		
☀	☁	☁	☁	☁	☁
❑	❑	❑	❑	❑	❑

Powerton Lake is a 1,426 acre cooling reservoir owned by Commonwealth Edison. Approximately 60% is open to waterfowl hunting. The remaining is maintained as a waterfowl rest area.

Check In:............................. Check Out:.............................

Lodging:.................................. Park hours:........................

Who I Went With:...

Fee(s):.. Will I Return? YES / NO

Rating

⭐ ⭐ ⭐ ⭐ ⭐

Activities

❑ ATV/OHV	❑ Horseback Riding	❑ Fishing	❑ Wildlife
❑ Berry Picking	❑ Kayaking	❑ Hiking	❑ Bird Viewing
❑ Biking	❑ Photography	❑ Hunting	❑ Snowmobiling
❑ Boating	❑ Skiing	❑ Snowshoeing	❑ ....
❑ Canoeing	❑ Skijoring	❑ Swimming	❑ ....

Facilities

❑ ADA	❑ Visitor Center	❑ Museum	❑ ....
❑ Gift Shop	❑ Picnic Sites	❑ Restrooms	❑ ....

Notes

....
....
....
....

Passport Stamps

PROPHETSTOWN STATE RECREATION AREA

Whiteside

DATE(S) VISITED:..

❑ SPRING ❑ SUMMER ❑ FALL ❑ WINTER

WEATHER	TEMP:

❑ ❑ ❑ ❑ ❑ ❑

Check In:............................. Check Out:.............................

Lodging:............................. Park hours:.......................

Who I Went With:...

Fee(s):... Will I Return? YES / NO

Rating ⭐ ⭐ ⭐ ⭐ ⭐

ABOUT THIS STATE PARK

Prophetstown State Park, on the northeast edge of Prophetstown along the south bank of the Rock River in Whiteside County, is a scenic and historic area offering a variety of recreational facilities. Once the site of an American Indian village, the 53-acre park derives its name from the Native American prophet Wa-bo-kie-shiek.

Activities

❑ ATV/OHV
❑ Berry Picking
❑ Biking
❑ Boating
❑ Canoeing

❑ Horseback Riding
❑ Kayaking
❑ Photography
❑ Skiing
❑ Skijoring

❑ Fishing
❑ Hiking
❑ Hunting
❑ Snowshoeing
❑ Swimming

❑ Wildlife
❑ Bird Viewing
❑ Snowmobiling
❑ ....
❑ ....

Facilities

❑ ADA
❑ Gift Shop

❑ Visitor Center
❑ Picnic Sites

❑ Museum
❑ Restrooms

❑ ....
❑ ....

Notes

....
....
....
....

Passport Stamps

PYRAMID STATE RECREATION AREA

Perry

DATE(S) VISITED:...

❑ SPRING   ❑ SUMMER   ❑ FALL   ❑ WINTER

WEATHER						TEMP:	

❑   ❑   ❑   ❑   ❑   ❑

ABOUT THIS STATE PARK

Pyramid State Recreation Area consists of forested hills, lakes and ponds. More than 500 acres of water form lakes varying in size from 0.1 acres to 276 acres offer outstanding fishing opportunities. The largest lake on the property, known as Super Lake, is located on the Captain Unit. Most of the lakes on the original Pyramid site were created prior to 1950. Since many of the lakes can be reached only by foot, Pyramid affords an opportunity for the angler to get away from crowds.

Check In:.............................. Check Out:..............................

Lodging:.................................. Park hours:.......................

Who I Went With:..

Fee(s):... Will I Return? YES / NO

Rating ⭐ ⭐ ⭐ ⭐ ⭐

Activities

❑ ATV/OHV   ❑ Horseback Riding   ❑ Fishing   ❑ Wildlife
❑ Berry Picking   ❑ Kayaking   ❑ Hiking   ❑ Bird Viewing
❑ Biking   ❑ Photography   ❑ Hunting   ❑ Snowmobiling
❑ Boating   ❑ Skiing   ❑ Snowshoeing   ❑ ....
❑ Canoeing   ❑ Skijoring   ❑ Swimming   ❑ ....

Facilities

❑ ADA   ❑ Visitor Center   ❑ Museum   ❑ ....
❑ Gift Shop   ❑ Picnic Sites   ❑ Restrooms   ❑ ....

Notes

....
....
....
....

Passport Stamps

RAMSEY LAKE STATE RECREATION AREA

Fayette

DATE(S) VISITED:..

❑ SPRING ❑ SUMMER ❑ FALL ❑ WINTER

WEATHER	TEMP:
☀ ❄ ☁ 🌧 🌧 🌨	
❑ ❑ ❑ ❑ ❑ ❑	

Check In:............................. Check Out:.............................

Lodging:................................... Park hours:........................

Who I Went With:...

Fee(s):.. Will I Return? YES / NO

Rating ⭐ ⭐ ⭐ ⭐ ⭐

ABOUT THIS STATE PARK

Rolling hills, timbered shoreline, and beautiful Ramsey Lake make the Ramsey Lake State Recreation Area a unique and popular recreation spot. Visitors will enjoy the picturesque woods, secluded picnic areas, and excellent fishing and hunting opportunities. Ramsey Lake SRA is the perfect place for people who want to relax or for those energetic outdoor types who want to hike, hunt, fish, or camp. The site is located just northwest of Ramsey in Fayette County.

Activities

❑ ATV/OHV
❑ Berry Picking
❑ Biking
❑ Boating
❑ Canoeing

❑ Horseback Riding
❑ Kayaking
❑ Photography
❑ Skiing
❑ Skijoring

❑ Fishing
❑ Hiking
❑ Hunting
❑ Snowshoeing
❑ Swimming

❑ Wildlife
❑ Bird Viewing
❑ Snowmobiling
❑ ....
❑ ....

Facilities

❑ ADA
❑ Gift Shop

❑ Visitor Center
❑ Picnic Sites

❑ Museum
❑ Restrooms

❑ ....
❑ ....

Notes

....
....
....
....

Passport Stamps

RANDOLPH COUNTY STATE RECREATION AREA

Randolph

DATE(S) VISITED:...

❑ SPRING   ❑ SUMMER   ❑ FALL   ❑ WINTER

WEATHER	TEMP:
☀ ❄☁ ☁ ☁ ☁ ☁	
❑ ❑ ❑ ❑ ❑ ❑	

Check In:............................ Check Out:...............................

Lodging:............................ Park hours:...............................

Who I Went With:...

Fee(s):.. Will I Return? YES / NO

Rating ⭐ ⭐ ⭐ ⭐ ⭐

ABOUT THIS STATE PARK

Randolph County State Recreation Area is a mecca for outdoor recreational activities. Fishing, hiking, picnicking, boating, hunting and camping are just a few of the choices on the 1,101 acres at the site. Located five miles northeast of Chester, Randolph County SRA lies in the rolling hill country of southern Illinois. Offering a cool retreat from hot summer days, well shaded picnic areas, hiking trails and scenic forest stands await park visitors.

Activities

❑ ATV/OHV	❑ Horseback Riding	❑ Fishing	❑ Wildlife
❑ Berry Picking	❑ Kayaking	❑ Hiking	❑ Bird Viewing
❑ Biking	❑ Photography	❑ Hunting	❑ Snowmobiling
❑ Boating	❑ Skiing	❑ Snowshoeing	❑ ....
❑ Canoeing	❑ Skijoring	❑ Swimming	❑ ....

Facilities

❑ ADA	❑ Visitor Center	❑ Museum	❑ ....
❑ Gift Shop	❑ Picnic Sites	❑ Restrooms	❑ ....

Notes

....
....
....
....

Passport Stamps

RAY NORBUT STATE FISH AND WILDLIFE AREA

Pike

DATE(S) VISITED:...

☐ SPRING   ☐ SUMMER   ☐ FALL   ☐ WINTER

WEATHER	TEMP:
☀ ☐ ❄☁ ☐ ☁ ☐ ☁|||| ☐ ☁⋰ ☐ ☁⋯ ☐	

Check In:............................. Check Out:...............................

Lodging:................................... Park hours:........................

Who I Went With:...

Fee(s):... Will I Return?   YES / NO

Rating ⭐ ⭐ ⭐ ⭐ ⭐

ABOUT THIS STATE PARK

Ray Norbut State Fish and Wildlife Area is a 1,140-acre mosaic of bottomlands, woodlands, wetlands, open fields, steep hills, rocky ravines, hollows, brushy draws and bluffs. Located along the Illinois River. Big Blue Island, a narrow, 100-acre strip of land in the river, is part of the site. Other notable geographic features are two west-east flowing streams--Blue Creek, a river tributary, and the spring-fed Napoleon Hollow Creek.

Activities

☐ ATV/OHV	☐ Horseback Riding	☐ Fishing	☐ Wildlife
☐ Berry Picking	☐ Kayaking	☐ Hiking	☐ Bird Viewing
☐ Biking	☐ Photography	☐ Hunting	☐ Snowmobiling
☐ Boating	☐ Skiing	☐ Snowshoeing	☐ ....
☐ Canoeing	☐ Skijoring	☐ Swimming	☐ ....

Facilities

☐ ADA	☐ Visitor Center	☐ Museum	☐ ....
☐ Gift Shop	☐ Picnic Sites	☐ Restrooms	☐ ....

Notes

....
....
....
....

Passport Stamps

RED HILLS STATE PARK

Lawrence

DATE(S) VISITED:..

☐ SPRING ☐ SUMMER ☐ FALL ☐ WINTER

ABOUT THIS STATE PARK

In southeastern Illinois midway between Olney and Lawrenceville on U.S. 50, Red Hills is a carefully preserved and maintained 967 acres of high wooded hills, deep ravines, captivating meadows and year-round springs. It's the perfect setting for natural relaxation and outdoor activities. The sparkling 40-acre lake is ideal for fishing and boating.
Pause to enjoy the spectacular scenic view from atop Red Hills--the highest point of land between St. Louis and Cincinnati.

WEATHER	TEMP:

☀ ☐   ❄☁ ☐   ☁ ☐   🌧 ☐   🌨 ☐   ☁ ☐

Check In:............................. Check Out:.............................

Lodging:.................................. Park hours:........................

Who I Went With:...

Fee(s):... Will I Return? YES / NO

Rating ★ ★ ★ ★ ★

Activities

☐ ATV/OHV   ☐ Horseback Riding   ☐ Fishing   ☐ Wildlife
☐ Berry Picking ☐ Kayaking   ☐ Hiking   ☐ Bird Viewing
☐ Biking   ☐ Photography   ☐ Hunting   ☐ Snowmobiling
☐ Boating   ☐ Skiing   ☐ Snowshoeing ☐ ....
☐ Canoeing   ☐ Skijoring   ☐ Swimming   ☐ ....

Facilities

☐ ADA   ☐ Visitor Center   ☐ Museum   ☐ ....
☐ Gift Shop   ☐ Picnic Sites   ☐ Restrooms   ☐ ....

Notes

....
....
....
....

Passport Stamps

REND LAKE STATE FISH AND WILDLIFE AREA

Franklin, Jefferson

DATE(S) VISITED:..

❏ SPRING   ❏ SUMMER   ❏ FALL   ❏ WINTER

WEATHER	TEMP:

☀ ❏   🌤 ❏   ☁ ❏   🌧 ❏   🌨 ❏   🌦 ❏

Check In:............................ Check Out:..............................

Lodging:.................................. Park hours:......................

Who I Went With:..

Fee(s):.. Will I Return?   YES / NO

Rating ★ ★ ★ ★ ★

ABOUT THIS STATE PARK

This area consists of bottomland hardwoods, upland ag fields, and surrounding land including 3,000 acres of impounded water in the sub-impoundments managed primarily for waterfowl. Food is produced both by tenant farming, site staff farming, and moist-soil production. Five thousand posted acres are managed as a waterfowl refuge. All areas are open to fishing most of the year with the refuge area being closed during waterfowl use periods.

Activities

❏ ATV/OHV	❏ Horseback Riding	❏ Fishing	❏ Wildlife
❏ Berry Picking	❏ Kayaking	❏ Hiking	❏ Bird Viewing
❏ Biking	❏ Photography	❏ Hunting	❏ Snowmobiling
❏ Boating	❏ Skiing	❏ Snowshoeing	❏ ....
❏ Canoeing	❏ Skijoring	❏ Swimming	❏ ....

Facilities

❏ ADA	❏ Visitor Center	❏ Museum	❏ ....
❏ Gift Shop	❏ Picnic Sites	❏ Restrooms	❏ ....

Notes

....
....
....
....

Passport Stamps

RICE LAKE STATE FISH AND WILDLIFE AREA

Fulton

DATE(S) VISITED:..

❏ SPRING ❏ SUMMER ❏ FALL ❏ WINTER

WEATHER					TEMP:
❏	❏	❏	❏	❏	❏

Check In:.............................. Check Out:...............................

Lodging:.................................. Park hours:...............................

Who I Went With:..

Fee(s):... Will I Return? YES / NO

Rating ★ ★ ★ ★ ★

ABOUT THIS STATE PARK

Providing a stop-over area for migrating waterfowl, Rice Lake and the surrounding areas provide an excellent opportunity for wildlife observation. Visitors may also sight he American bald eagle, which uses the bottomland timber for roosting. Fishing is a favorite pastime at the area, with seasonal fluctuations of the water levels, fishing may be limited during certain times of the year. Duck hunting and archery deer hunting also provide opportunities for the outdoor sportsman.

Activities

❏ ATV/OHV	❏ Horseback Riding	❏ Fishing	❏ Wildlife
❏ Berry Picking	❏ Kayaking	❏ Hiking	❏ Bird Viewing
❏ Biking	❏ Photography	❏ Hunting	❏ Snowmobiling
❏ Boating	❏ Skiing	❏ Snowshoeing	❏ ....
❏ Canoeing	❏ Skijoring	❏ Swimming	❏ ....

Facilities

❏ ADA	❏ Visitor Center	❏ Museum	❏ ....
❏ Gift Shop	❏ Picnic Sites	❏ Restrooms	❏ ....

Notes

....
....
....
....

Passport Stamps

ROCK CUT STATE PARK

DATE(S) VISITED:..

❑ SPRING ❑ SUMMER ❑ FALL ❑ WINTER

WEATHER	TEMP:

❑ ❑ ❑ ❑ ❑ ❑

Check In:............................... Check Out:.............................

Lodging:................................. Park hours:........................

Who I Went With:...

Fee(s):.. Will I Return? YES / NO

Rating ⭐ ⭐ ⭐ ⭐ ⭐

ABOUT THIS STATE PARK

Rock Cut's 3,092 acres include two lakes: Pierce Lake, with 162 acres, and Olson Lake with 50 acres offer a retreat for people wanting to fish, ice fish or ice skate. The park's hiking trails, horseback riding trails and cross-country skiing and wildlife watching, as well as seasonal hunting programs, make it a year round recreation destination. The beautiful campground has 270 premium campsites, a rustic cabin, a youth group camp and shelters.

Activities

❑ ATV/OHV	❑ Horseback Riding	❑ Fishing	❑ Wildlife
❑ Berry Picking	❑ Kayaking	❑ Hiking	❑ Bird Viewing
❑ Biking	❑ Photography	❑ Hunting	❑ Snowmobiling
❑ Boating	❑ Skiing	❑ Snowshoeing	❑ ....
❑ Canoeing	❑ Skijoring	❑ Swimming	❑ ....

Facilities

❑ ADA	❑ Visitor Center	❑ Museum	❑ ....
❑ Gift Shop	❑ Picnic Sites	❑ Restrooms	❑ ....

Notes

....

....

....

....

Passport Stamps

ROCK ISLAND TRAIL STATE PARK

Stark, Peoria

DATE(S) VISITED:..

❑ SPRING ❑ SUMMER ❑ FALL ❑ WINTER

WEATHER			TEMP:		
❑	❑	❑	❑	❑	❑

ABOUT THIS STATE PARK

Beauty and solitude, away from the hustle and bustle of city traffic, await visitors at Rock Island Trail State Park. Stretching for 26 miles from Alta, in Peoria County, to Toulon, in Stark County, the park offers many natural and architectural attractions in a tree-canopied corridor that is only 50 to 100 feet wide. Prairie grasses and wildflowers co-exist as remnants of early rail travel along the trail. Just north of Alta, an arched culvert provides a lovely backdrop for the natural beauty of the area.

Check In:............................. Check Out:..............................

Lodging:................................... Park hours:.......................

Who I Went With:..

Fee(s):.. Will I Return? YES / NO

Rating ⭐ ⭐ ⭐ ⭐ ⭐

Activities

❑ ATV/OHV	❑ Horseback Riding	❑ Fishing	❑ Wildlife
❑ Berry Picking	❑ Kayaking	❑ Hiking	❑ Bird Viewing
❑ Biking	❑ Photography	❑ Hunting	❑ Snowmobiling
❑ Boating	❑ Skiing	❑ Snowshoeing	❑ ....
❑ Canoeing	❑ Skijoring	❑ Swimming	❑ ....

Facilities

❑ ADA	❑ Visitor Center	❑ Museum	❑ ....
❑ Gift Shop	❑ Picnic Sites	❑ Restrooms	❑ ....

Notes

....

....

....

....

Passport Stamps

SALINE COUNTY STATE FISH AND WILDLIFE AREA

Saline

DATE(S) VISITED:...

❏ SPRING   ❏ SUMMER   ❏ FALL   ❏ WINTER

WEATHER			TEMP:		
☀	☁	☁	☁	☁	☁
❏	❏	❏	❏	❏	❏

Check In:............................. Check Out:...............................

Lodging:.................................. Park hours:........................

Who I Went With:...

Fee(s):.. Will I Return?   YES / NO

Rating ⭐ ⭐ ⭐ ⭐ ⭐

ABOUT THIS STATE PARK

Saline County State Fish & Wildlife Area, 5 miles southeast of Equality in southeastern Illinois, was the site of springs and wells that furnished brine for one of the two salt works. Although the springs and wells are not visible today, the area primarily is a recreational site. The initial acquisition of 524 acres of land was made in 1959 by the state of Illinois, and the total acreage now totals 1,270 acres, including a beautiful 105-acre lake.

Activities

❏ ATV/OHV	❏ Horseback Riding	❏ Fishing	❏ Wildlife
❏ Berry Picking	❏ Kayaking	❏ Hiking	❏ Bird Viewing
❏ Biking	❏ Photography	❏ Hunting	❏ Snowmobiling
❏ Boating	❏ Skiing	❏ Snowshoeing	❏ ....
❏ Canoeing	❏ Skijoring	❏ Swimming	❏ ....

Facilities

❏ ADA	❏ Visitor Center	❏ Museum	❏ ....
❏ Gift Shop	❏ Picnic Sites	❏ Restrooms	❏ ....

Notes

....
....
....
....

Passport Stamps

SAM DALE LAKE STATE FISH AND WILDLIFE AREA

Wayne

DATE(S) VISITED:...

☐ SPRING   ☐ SUMMER   ☐ FALL   ☐ WINTER

WEATHER						TEMP:
☀	❄☁	☁	☁	☁	☁	
☐	☐	☐	☐	☐	☐	

Check In:............................ Check Out:..............................

Lodging:.................................. Park hours:........................

Who I Went With:...

Fee(s):... Will I Return?   YES / NO

ABOUT THIS STATE PARK

Gently rolling terrain, lush woods and a beautiful lake make the Sam Dale Lake State Fish and Wildlife Area the perfect spot for a family outing. This area has something for everyone: fishing, hunting, picnicking, and camping. The highlight of a visit is the Sam Dale Lake, a beautiful 194-acre lake with 5 miles of shoreline trails to enjoy or explore. In addition, several smaller ponds are home to fish and wildlife.

Rating ⭐ ⭐ ⭐ ⭐ ⭐

Activities

☐ ATV/OHV	☐ Horseback Riding	☐ Fishing	☐ Wildlife
☐ Berry Picking	☐ Kayaking	☐ Hiking	☐ Bird Viewing
☐ Biking	☐ Photography	☐ Hunting	☐ Snowmobiling
☐ Boating	☐ Skiing	☐ Snowshoeing	☐ ....
☐ Canoeing	☐ Skijoring	☐ Swimming	☐ ....

Facilities

☐ ADA	☐ Visitor Center	☐ Museum	☐ ....
☐ Gift Shop	☐ Picnic Sites	☐ Restrooms	☐ ....

Notes

....
....
....
....

Passport Stamps

SAM PARR STATE FISH AND WILDLIFE AREA

Jasper

DATE(S) VISITED:..

❏ SPRING   ❏ SUMMER   ❏ FALL   ❏ WINTER

WEATHER			TEMP:		
☀	⛅	☁	🌧	🌨	🌧
❏	❏	❏	❏	❏	❏

Check In:............................ Check Out:...............................

Lodging:.................................. Park hours:........................

Who I Went With:...

Fee(s):... Will I Return?   YES / NO

Rating ⭐ ⭐ ⭐ ⭐ ⭐

ABOUT THIS STATE PARK

For several decades the residents of Jasper County worked for a state park, assisted and encouraged by a former resident and conservationist, Sam Parr. In 1960, 72 acres of land approximately 3 miles northeast of Newton were acquired by the Department of Natural Resources and the Jasper County Conservation Area became a reality. Additional acquisitions have brought the total acreage to 1,180, including a 183-acre lake.

Activities

❏ ATV/OHV	❏ Horseback Riding	❏ Fishing	❏ Wildlife
❏ Berry Picking	❏ Kayaking	❏ Hiking	❏ Bird Viewing
❏ Biking	❏ Photography	❏ Hunting	❏ Snowmobiling
❏ Boating	❏ Skiing	❏ Snowshoeing	❏ ....
❏ Canoeing	❏ Skijoring	❏ Swimming	❏ ....

Facilities

❏ ADA	❏ Visitor Center	❏ Museum	❏ ....
❏ Gift Shop	❏ Picnic Sites	❏ Restrooms	❏ ....

Notes

....
....
....
....

Passport Stamps

SAND RIDGE STATE FOREST

Mason

DATE(S) VISITED:..

❑ SPRING ❑ SUMMER ❑ FALL ❑ WINTER

WEATHER	TEMP:
☀ ❄☁ ☁ 🌧 🌨 🌦	
❑ ❑ ❑ ❑ ❑ ❑	

Check In:............................. Check Out:..............................

Lodging:.................................. Park hours:........................

Who I Went With:..

Fee(s):.. Will I Return? YES / NO

Rating
⭐ ⭐ ⭐ ⭐ ⭐

ABOUT THIS STATE PARK

For those who think central Illinois is one big corn field, Sand Ridge State Forest will come as a pleasant surprise. The forest is an island in a sea of agriculture. This 7,200-acre forest, the largest of Illinois' state forests, boasts sweeping expanses of native oak-hickory woodland, extensive pine plantations, sprawling open fields, grasslands and completely unique sand prairies. For a refreshing, invigorating taste of unspoiled nature and an opportunity to experience truly unique environment, Sand Ridge State Forest is ideal.

Activities

❑ ATV/OHV	❑ Horseback Riding	❑ Fishing	❑ Wildlife
❑ Berry Picking	❑ Kayaking	❑ Hiking	❑ Bird Viewing
❑ Biking	❑ Photography	❑ Hunting	❑ Snowmobiling
❑ Boating	❑ Skiing	❑ Snowshoeing	❑ ....
❑ Canoeing	❑ Skijoring	❑ Swimming	❑ ....

Facilities

❑ ADA	❑ Visitor Center	❑ Museum	❑ ....
❑ Gift Shop	❑ Picnic Sites	❑ Restrooms	❑ ....

Notes
....
....
....
....

Passport Stamps

SANGANOIS STATE FISH AND WILDLIFE AREA

Cass, Schuyler, Mason

DATE(S) VISITED:...

❑ SPRING ❑ SUMMER ❑ FALL ❑ WINTER

WEATHER				TEMP:	
❑	❑	❑	❑	❑	❑

Check In:............................. Check Out:.............................

Lodging:................................... Park hours:........................

Who I Went With:...

Fee(s):.. Will I Return? YES / NO

Rating ⭐ ⭐ ⭐ ⭐ ⭐

ABOUT THIS STATE PARK

The Sanganois State Fish and Wildlife Area is primarily a waterfowl management area. The site offers waterfowl, forest game and furbearer hunting with limited upland game opportunities. . The area is a typical bottomland complex of sloughs, backwater lakes, timbered ponds, and bottomland timber. Waterfowl hunting is restricted to marked blind sites and a designated walk-in area. There are approximately 60 blind sites which are drawn for on an annual basis; also approximately 500 acres are open to walk-in hunting.

Activities

❑ ATV/OHV	❑ Horseback Riding	❑ Fishing	❑ Wildlife
❑ Berry Picking	❑ Kayaking	❑ Hiking	❑ Bird Viewing
❑ Biking	❑ Photography	❑ Hunting	❑ Snowmobiling
❑ Boating	❑ Skiing	❑ Snowshoeing	❑ ....
❑ Canoeing	❑ Skijoring	❑ Swimming	❑ ....

Facilities

❑ ADA	❑ Visitor Center	❑ Museum	❑ ....
❑ Gift Shop	❑ Picnic Sites	❑ Restrooms	❑ ....

Notes

....
....
....
....

Passport Stamps

SANGCHRIS LAKE STATE RECREATION AREA

DATE(S) VISITED:..

☐ SPRING ☐ SUMMER ☐ FALL ☐ WINTER

WEATHER			TEMP:		
☐	☐	☐	☐	☐	☐

Check In:............................ Check Out:............................

Lodging:.................................. Park hours:.......................

Who I Went With:...

Fee(s):.. Will I Return? YES / NO

Rating ⭐⭐⭐⭐⭐

ABOUT THIS STATE PARK

Located minutes southeast of Springfield, Sangchris Lake State Park serves as a perfect home-base for enjoying outdoor activities including fishing, boating, camping, hunting, picnics and family gatherings amid native forests of oak, maple, butternut and persimmon. The park totals more than 3,000 acres, with 120 miles of shoreline on Sangchris Lake, a power station cooling lake constructed in 1964. Camping is available near the lakeshore at the Deer Run and Hickory Point campgrounds.

Activities

☐ ATV/OHV	☐ Horseback Riding	☐ Fishing	☐ Wildlife
☐ Berry Picking	☐ Kayaking	☐ Hiking	☐ Bird Viewing
☐ Biking	☐ Photography	☐ Hunting	☐ Snowmobiling
☐ Boating	☐ Skiing	☐ Snowshoeing	☐ ....
☐ Canoeing	☐ Skijoring	☐ Swimming	☐ ....

Facilities

☐ ADA	☐ Visitor Center	☐ Museum	☐ ....
☐ Gift Shop	☐ Picnic Sites	☐ Restrooms	☐ ....

Notes

....
....
....
....

Passport Stamps

SHABBONA LAKE STATE PARK

DeKalb

DATE(S) VISITED:..

❏ SPRING ❏ SUMMER ❏ FALL ❏ WINTER

ABOUT THIS STATE PARK

Just miles west of Chicago, off U.S. 30, urban landscape gives way to 1,550 acres of rolling prairie and a 318.8-acre man-made fishing lake. Shabbona Lake State Recreation Area provides a convenient, natural haven from the hustle and bustle of daily life. With facilities for picnicking, camping, hiking, fishing, hunting and winter sports, Shabbona Lake SRA is a convenient and comfortable retreat where visitors can refresh and reinvigorate in a rare, unspoiled environment.

WEATHER	TEMP:

❏ ☀ ❏ 🌤 ❏ ☁ ❏ 🌧 ❏ 🌨 ❏ 🌦

Check In:................................ Check Out:................................

Lodging:.................................. Park hours:........................

Who I Went With:..

Fee(s):....................................... Will I Return? YES / NO

Rating ★ ★ ★ ★ ★

Activities

❏ ATV/OHV
❏ Berry Picking
❏ Biking
❏ Boating
❏ Canoeing

❏ Horseback Riding
❏ Kayaking
❏ Photography
❏ Skiing
❏ Skijoring

❏ Fishing
❏ Hiking
❏ Hunting
❏ Snowshoeing
❏ Swimming

❏ Wildlife
❏ Bird Viewing
❏ Snowmobiling
❏ ....
❏ ....

Facilities

❏ ADA
❏ Gift Shop

❏ Visitor Center
❏ Picnic Sites

❏ Museum
❏ Restrooms

❏ ....
❏ ....

Notes

....
....
....
....

Passport Stamps

SHELBYVILLE STATE FISH AND WILDLIFE AREA

Moultrie

DATE(S) VISITED:...

❑ SPRING ❑ SUMMER ❑ FALL ❑ WINTER

WEATHER	TEMP:

❑ ❑ ❑ ❑ ❑ ❑

ABOUT THIS STATE PARK

Located along the Kaskaskia and West Okaw rivers near Sullivan, the Shelbyville State Fish and Wildlife Area offers some of the best hunting, river fishing, and nature study opportunities in Illinois. The area contains more than 6,000 acres of mixed habitats including forests, prairies, restored grasslands, old fields, brush, wetlands, rivers, streams and cropland in the upper reaches of the 34,000-acre Lake Shelbyville project area.

Check In:............................. Check Out:...............................

Lodging:.................................. Park hours:........................

Who I Went With:...

Fee(s):... Will I Return? YES / NO

Rating ⭐ ⭐ ⭐ ⭐ ⭐

Activities

❑ ATV/OHV	❑ Horseback Riding	❑ Fishing	❑ Wildlife
❑ Berry Picking	❑ Kayaking	❑ Hiking	❑ Bird Viewing
❑ Biking	❑ Photography	❑ Hunting	❑ Snowmobiling
❑ Boating	❑ Skiing	❑ Snowshoeing	❑ ....
❑ Canoeing	❑ Skijoring	❑ Swimming	❑ ....

Facilities

❑ ADA	❑ Visitor Center	❑ Museum	❑ ....
❑ Gift Shop	❑ Picnic Sites	❑ Restrooms	❑ ....

Notes

....
....
....
....

Passport Stamps

DATE(S) VISITED:..

❏ SPRING ❏ SUMMER ❏ FALL ❏ WINTER

WEATHER			TEMP:		
❏	❏	❏	❏	❏	❏

Check In:............................ Check Out:...............................

Lodging:.................................. Park hours:........................

Who I Went With:...

Fee(s):... Will I Return? YES / NO

Rating ★ ★ ★ ★ ★

ABOUT THIS STATE PARK

Within the 385-acre Sielbeck Land and Water Reserve occurs 110 acres of high-quality wet-mesic floodplain forest dominated by cherrybark oak, sweetgum and pin oak. Hidden within the surrounding soggy forest is 35 acres of forested swamp dominated by cypress and tupelo. Many of the trees are 200 years old and nearly 4 feet in diameter. Another common sight in ancient timber is an abundance of dead and dying trees.

Activities

❏ ATV/OHV	❏ Horseback Riding	❏ Fishing	❏ Wildlife
❏ Berry Picking	❏ Kayaking	❏ Hiking	❏ Bird Viewing
❏ Biking	❏ Photography	❏ Hunting	❏ Snowmobiling
❏ Boating	❏ Skiing	❏ Snowshoeing	❏ ....
❏ Canoeing	❏ Skijoring	❏ Swimming	❏ ....

Facilities

❏ ADA	❏ Visitor Center	❏ Museum	❏ ....
❏ Gift Shop	❏ Picnic Sites	❏ Restrooms	❏ ....

Notes

....
....
....
....

Passport Stamps

SILOAM SPRINGS STATE PARK

Adams, Brown

DATE(S) VISITED:..

❑ SPRING ❑ SUMMER ❑ FALL ❑ WINTER

WEATHER	TEMP:
☀ ❄ ☁ ☁ ☔ ☁	
❑ ❑ ❑ ❑ ❑ ❑	

Check In:............................. Check Out:...........................

Lodging:.................................... Park hours:.......................

Who I Went With:...

Fee(s):.. Will I Return? YES / NO

Rating ★ ★ ★ ★ ★

ABOUT THIS STATE PARK

The beautifully wooded terrain, sparkling lake and carefully maintained facilities make this 3,323-acre site one of the most beautiful parks in Illinois. It's an ideal setting for outdoor visits, whether your interest is hunting, fishing, camping, boating, picnicking, hiking or bird watching. The park is surrounded by luxuriantly forested gullies and scenic crests alive with wild roses, black-eyed Susans, white false indigo, and snapdragons.

Activities

❑ ATV/OHV	❑ Horseback Riding	❑ Fishing	❑ Wildlife
❑ Berry Picking	❑ Kayaking	❑ Hiking	❑ Bird Viewing
❑ Biking	❑ Photography	❑ Hunting	❑ Snowmobiling
❑ Boating	❑ Skiing	❑ Snowshoeing	❑ ....
❑ Canoeing	❑ Skijoring	❑ Swimming	❑ ....

Facilities

❑ ADA	❑ Visitor Center	❑ Museum	❑ ....
❑ Gift Shop	❑ Picnic Sites	❑ Restrooms	❑ ....

Notes

....
....
....
....

Passport Stamps

SILVER SPRINGS STATE FISH & WILDLIFE AREA

Kendall

DATE(S) VISITED:..

❏ SPRING   ❏ SUMMER   ❏ FALL   ❏ WINTER

WEATHER	TEMP:
☀ ❏ 🌤 ❏ ☁ ❏ 🌧 ❏ 🌧 ❏ 🌨 ❏	

Check In:.............................. Check Out:..............................

Lodging:................................. Park hours:.......................

Who I Went With:...

Fee(s):.. Will I Return? YES / NO

Rating ⭐ ⭐ ⭐ ⭐ ⭐

ABOUT THIS STATE PARK

Which is home to several small manmade lakes. A natural prairie restoration project gives visitors a feeling of the original landscape with native wildflowers, songbirds, waterfowl and upland game. Picnicking, fishing and hiking are popular pastimes in summer, with ice fishing, sledding, ice skating and cross-country ski trails available for the winter sports lover. For relaxing, exercising or just enjoying nature, Silver Springs is the perfect getaway location.

Activities

❏ ATV/OHV   ❏ Horseback Riding   ❏ Fishing   ❏ Wildlife
❏ Berry Picking   ❏ Kayaking   ❏ Hiking   ❏ Bird Viewing
❏ Biking   ❏ Photography   ❏ Hunting   ❏ Snowmobiling
❏ Boating   ❏ Skiing   ❏ Snowshoeing   ❏ ....
❏ Canoeing   ❏ Skijoring   ❏ Swimming   ❏ ....

Facilities

❏ ADA   ❏ Visitor Center   ❏ Museum   ❏ ....
❏ Gift Shop   ❏ Picnic Sites   ❏ Restrooms   ❏ ....

Notes

....
....
....
....

Passport Stamps

SNAKEDEN HOLLOW STATE FISH AND WILDLIFE AREA

Knox

DATE(S) VISITED:..

❏ SPRING ❏ SUMMER ❏ FALL ❏ WINTER

ABOUT THIS STATE PARK

The site contains 125 water impoundments totaling 400 acres. All lakes and ponds, except the 160-acre Snakeden Hollow Lake, were formed as the result of surface mining operations. The water areas currently contain largemouth and smallmouth bass, rainbow and brown trout and muskie.Good wildlife habitat provides a home to numerous species of mammals, birds and reptiles. A favorite nesting spot of giant Canada geese, the site has 2,100 acres of grassland, brushy draws, briers, shrubs, cropland and limited hardwood forest.

WEATHER			TEMP:		
❏	❏	❏	❏	❏	❏

Check In:............................. Check Out:..............................

Lodging:.................................... Park hours:.......................

Who I Went With:...

Fee(s):... Will I Return?   YES / NO

Rating ★ ★ ★ ★ ★

Activities

❏ ATV/OHV
❏ Berry Picking
❏ Biking
❏ Boating
❏ Canoeing

❏ Horseback Riding
❏ Kayaking
❏ Photography
❏ Skiing
❏ Skijoring

❏ Fishing
❏ Hiking
❏ Hunting
❏ Snowshoeing
❏ Swimming

❏ Wildlife
❏ Bird Viewing
❏ Snowmobiling
❏ ....
❏ ....

Facilities

❏ ADA
❏ Gift Shop

❏ Visitor Center
❏ Picnic Sites

❏ Museum
❏ Restrooms

❏ ....
❏ ....

Notes

....
....
....
....

Passport Stamps

SPITLER WOODS STATE NATURAL AREA

Macon

DATE(S) VISITED:..

❑ SPRING   ❑ SUMMER   ❑ FALL   ❑ WINTER

WEATHER					
☀	❄☁	☁	☁🌧	☁	☁
❑	❑	❑	❑	❑	❑

TEMP:

ABOUT THIS STATE PARK

Spitler Woods State Natural Area, a 200-acre site in Mt. Zion in Macon County, is home to one of the largest acreages of old growth woods in central Illinois. Much of the site is dedicated as Spitler Woods Nature Preserve, providing additional protection for the site's valuable natural features. Spitler Woods provides outstanding habitat for songbirds, with birders spotting yellow-billed cuckoo, gray catbird, eastern wood pewee and red-bellied woodpecker.

Check In:............................. Check Out:................................

Lodging:.................................. Park hours:........................

Who I Went With:..

Fee(s):... Will I Return?   YES / NO

Rating ⭐ ⭐ ⭐ ⭐ ⭐

Activities

❑ ATV/OHV	❑ Horseback Riding	❑ Fishing	❑ Wildlife
❑ Berry Picking	❑ Kayaking	❑ Hiking	❑ Bird Viewing
❑ Biking	❑ Photography	❑ Hunting	❑ Snowmobiling
❑ Boating	❑ Skiing	❑ Snowshoeing	❑ ....
❑ Canoeing	❑ Skijoring	❑ Swimming	❑ ....

Facilities

❑ ADA	❑ Visitor Center	❑ Museum	❑ ....
❑ Gift Shop	❑ Picnic Sites	❑ Restrooms	❑ ....

Notes

....

....

....

....

Passport Stamps

SPRING LAKE FISH AND WILDLIFE AREA

Tazewell

DATE(S) VISITED:..

❑ SPRING   ❑ SUMMER   ❑ FALL   ❑ WINTER

WEATHER			TEMP:		
☀	❄☁	☁	☁	☁	☁
❑	❑	❑	❑	❑	❑

Check In:............................. Check Out:.............................

Lodging:............................... Park hours:.......................

Who I Went With:...

Fee(s):................................. Will I Return? YES / NO

Rating ★ ★ ★ ★ ★

ABOUT THIS STATE PARK

The lake lies almost parallel to the Illinois river for 8.5 miles up the river bottoms along the base of the river's east bluff. Spring Lake was described as a meander by an 1840 survey, and title was given to the State of Illinois. Overlooked by a large sandstone bluff, Spring Lake is a long, narrow lake created by a meander of the Illinois River. The lake covers an area of 1,285 acres, has a maximum depth of 10 feet and has 18 miles of shoreline.

Activities

❑ ATV/OHV	❑ Horseback Riding	❑ Fishing	❑ Wildlife
❑ Berry Picking	❑ Kayaking	❑ Hiking	❑ Bird Viewing
❑ Biking	❑ Photography	❑ Hunting	❑ Snowmobiling
❑ Boating	❑ Skiing	❑ Snowshoeing	❑ ....
❑ Canoeing	❑ Skijoring	❑ Swimming	❑ ....

Facilities

❑ ADA	❑ Visitor Center	❑ Museum	❑ ....
❑ Gift Shop	❑ Picnic Sites	❑ Restrooms	❑ ....

Notes

....
....
....
....

Passport Stamps

STARVED ROCK STATE PARK

LaSalle

DATE(S) VISITED:..

❑ SPRING ❑ SUMMER ❑ FALL ❑ WINTER

WEATHER			TEMP:		
☀ ❑	☁ ❑	☁ ❑	☔ ❑	☁ ❑	☁ ❑

Check In:............................. Check Out:...............................

Lodging:.................................. Park hours:........................

Who I Went With:...

Fee(s):... Will I Return? YES / NO

Rating ★ ★ ★ ★ ★

ABOUT THIS STATE PARK

Characterized by the many canyons within its 2,630 acres. Located just southeast of the village of Utica, in Deer Park Township, LaSalle County, Illinois, along the south bank of the Illinois River. A flood from a melting glacier, known as the Kankakee Torrent, which took place approximately 14,000–19,000 years ago led to the topography of the site and its exposed rock canyons. Diverse forest plant life exists in the park and the area supports several wild animal species. Of particular interest has been sport fishing species.

Activities

❑ ATV/OHV	❑ Horseback Riding	❑ Fishing	❑ Wildlife
❑ Berry Picking	❑ Kayaking	❑ Hiking	❑ Bird Viewing
❑ Biking	❑ Photography	❑ Hunting	❑ Snowmobiling
❑ Boating	❑ Skiing	❑ Snowshoeing	❑ ....
❑ Canoeing	❑ Skijoring	❑ Swimming	❑ ....

Facilities

❑ ADA	❑ Visitor Center	❑ Museum	❑ ....
❑ Gift Shop	❑ Picnic Sites	❑ Restrooms	❑ ....

Notes

....

....

....

....

Passport Stamps

STEPHEN A. FORBES STATE RECREATION AREA

Marion

DATE(S) VISITED:...

❑ SPRING   ❑ SUMMER   ❑ FALL   ❑ WINTER

WEATHER	TEMP:

☀ ❄☁ ☁ ☁▥ ☁☇ ☁⋯
❑   ❑   ❑   ❑   ❑   ❑

Check In:............................ Check Out:.............................

Lodging:.................................. Park hours:........................

Who I Went With:...

Fee(s):.. Will I Return?   YES / NO

Rating
⭐ ⭐ ⭐ ⭐ ⭐

ABOUT THIS STATE PARK

Picture yourself on the banks of a beautiful lake, surrounded by shady oaks and rolling hills. The presence of a graceful heron on the water, or deer or even a wild turkey in the nearby brush may be visible. Take a swim at sandy Rocky Point Beach. The rest of the day offers many options, from hiking on the nature trails, to softball or volleyball at the Circle Drive Picnic Area to water skiing. Or, you may want to spend the night at the Oak Ridge Campground. All of this, and more, awaits visitors to Stephen A. Forbes State Recreation Area.

Activities

❑ ATV/OHV   ❑ Horseback Riding   ❑ Fishing   ❑ Wildlife
❑ Berry Picking   ❑ Kayaking   ❑ Hiking   ❑ Bird Viewing
❑ Biking   ❑ Photography   ❑ Hunting   ❑ Snowmobiling
❑ Boating   ❑ Skiing   ❑ Snowshoeing   ❑ ....
❑ Canoeing   ❑ Skijoring   ❑ Swimming   ❑ ....

Facilities

❑ ADA   ❑ Visitor Center   ❑ Museum   ❑ ....
❑ Gift Shop   ❑ Picnic Sites   ❑ Restrooms   ❑ ....

Notes

....
....
....
....

Passport Stamps

TEN MILE CREEK STATE FISH & WILDLIFE AREA

Hamilton, Jeffersn

DATE(S) VISITED:..

❑ SPRING   ❑ SUMMER   ❑ FALL   ❑ WINTER

WEATHER	TEMP:
☀ ❄ ☁ 🌧 🌧 🌨	
❑ ❑ ❑ ❑ ❑ ❑	

ABOUT THIS STATE PARK

The Ten Mile Creek State Fish and Wildlife Area, located in southeastern Jefferson County and the western sections of Hamilton County, provides a wide range of outdoor recreation opportunities, including wildlife viewing, hiking, fishing, target shooting, hunting and trapping. Access to the site can be gained from rural roads leading from Illinois Route 142 and Illinois Route 14.

Check In:............................. Check Out:...............................

Lodging:.................................. Park hours:.......................

Who I Went With:...

Fee(s):... Will I Return? YES / NO

Rating ★★★★★

Activities

❑ ATV/OHV   ❑ Horseback Riding   ❑ Fishing   ❑ Wildlife
❑ Berry Picking   ❑ Kayaking   ❑ Hiking   ❑ Bird Viewing
❑ Biking   ❑ Photography   ❑ Hunting   ❑ Snowmobiling
❑ Boating   ❑ Skiing   ❑ Snowshoeing   ❑ ....
❑ Canoeing   ❑ Skijoring   ❑ Swimming   ❑ ....

Facilities

❑ ADA   ❑ Visitor Center   ❑ Museum   ❑ ....
❑ Gift Shop   ❑ Picnic Sites   ❑ Restrooms   ❑ ....

Notes

....
....
....
....

Passport Stamps

TRAIL OF TEARS STATE FOREST

Union

DATE(S) VISITED:..

☐ SPRING   ☐ SUMMER   ☐ FALL   ☐ WINTER

WEATHER				TEMP:	
☐	☐	☐	☐	☐	☐

ABOUT THIS STATE PARK

Trail of Tears State Forest is situated in western Union County, five miles northwest of Jonesboro and 20 miles south of Murphysboro. Just over 5,000 acres are within the state forest. The state forest system in Illinois was established to set aside lands for the growing of timber needed in production of forest products, for watershed protection, and to provide outdoor recreation. Trail of Tears State Forest is a multiple-use site managed for timber, wildlife, ecosystem preservation, watershed protection and recreation.

Check In:............................. Check Out:.............................

Lodging:............................. Park hours:.............................

Who I Went With:...

Fee(s):... Will I Return?   YES / NO

Rating ⭐ ⭐ ⭐ ⭐ ⭐

Activities

☐ ATV/OHV   ☐ Horseback Riding   ☐ Fishing   ☐ Wildlife
☐ Berry Picking   ☐ Kayaking   ☐ Hiking   ☐ Bird Viewing
☐ Biking   ☐ Photography   ☐ Hunting   ☐ Snowmobiling
☐ Boating   ☐ Skiing   ☐ Snowshoeing   ☐ ....
☐ Canoeing   ☐ Skijoring   ☐ Swimming   ☐ ....

Facilities

☐ ADA   ☐ Visitor Center   ☐ Museum   ☐ ....
☐ Gift Shop   ☐ Picnic Sites   ☐ Restrooms   ☐ ....

Notes
....
....
....
....

Passport Stamps

TUNNEL HILL STATE TRAIL

DATE(S) VISITED:..

❏ SPRING ❏ SUMMER ❏ FALL ❏ WINTER

WEATHER	TEMP:
☀ ❅☁ ☁ ☁||||| ☁🌧 ☁❄	
❏ ❏ ❏ ❏ ❏ ❏	

Tunnel Hill State Trail stretches for 45 miles from Harrisburg to Karnak. The trail continues on a trails spur for 2.5 miles from Karnak to Cache River State Natural Area - Henry Barkhausen Wetlands Center on the old Chicago and Eastern Illinois railroad bed. The 9.3-mile section between Tunnel Hill and Vienna crosses trails already known to outdoor recreationists: the River-to-River Trails, which extends from the Mississippi to the Ohio River; the unmarked American Discovery Trails.

Check In:................................ Check Out:...............................

Lodging:................................ Park hours:........................

Who I Went With:..

Fee(s):... Will I Return? YES / NO

Rating ⭐ ⭐ ⭐ ⭐ ⭐

Activities

❏ ATV/OHV	❏ Horseback Riding	❏ Fishing	❏ Wildlife
❏ Berry Picking	❏ Kayaking	❏ Hiking	❏ Bird Viewing
❏ Biking	❏ Photography	❏ Hunting	❏ Snowmobiling
❏ Boating	❏ Skiing	❏ Snowshoeing	❏ ....
❏ Canoeing	❏ Skijoring	❏ Swimming	❏ ....

Facilities

❏ ADA	❏ Visitor Center	❏ Museum	❏ ....
❏ Gift Shop	❏ Picnic Sites	❏ Restrooms	❏ ....

Notes

....
....
....
....

Passport Stamps

TURKEY BLUFFS STATE FISH AND WILDLIFE AREA

Randolph

DATE(S) VISITED:..

❑ SPRING   ❑ SUMMER   ❑ FALL   ❑ WINTER

WEATHER			TEMP:		
☀	❄☁	☁	☁	☁	☁
❑	❑	❑	❑	❑	❑

Check In:............................. Check Out:.............................

Lodging:................................. Park hours:........................

Who I Went With:..

Fee(s):... Will I Return?   YES / NO

Rating ⭐ ⭐ ⭐ ⭐ ⭐

ABOUT THIS STATE PARK

Located on the Mississippi River bluffs in southwestern Illinois. The topography varies from level flood plains to steep hills. Cultivated fields, along with hay fields and brushy areas, are interspersed with extensive stands of mature bottomland and upland timber.

Activities

❑ ATV/OHV	❑ Horseback Riding	❑ Fishing	❑ Wildlife
❑ Berry Picking	❑ Kayaking	❑ Hiking	❑ Bird Viewing
❑ Biking	❑ Photography	❑ Hunting	❑ Snowmobiling
❑ Boating	❑ Skiing	❑ Snowshoeing	❑ ....
❑ Canoeing	❑ Skijoring	❑ Swimming	❑ ....

Facilities

❑ ADA	❑ Visitor Center	❑ Museum	❑ ....
❑ Gift Shop	❑ Picnic Sites	❑ Restrooms	❑ ....

Notes

....
....
....
....

Passport Stamps

UNION COUNTY STATE FISH AND WILDLIFE AREA

Union

DATE(S) VISITED:...

☐ SPRING ☐ SUMMER ☐ FALL ☐ WINTER

WEATHER	TEMP:
☀ ❄ ☁ 🌧 🌦 🌨	
☐ ☐ ☐ ☐ ☐ ☐	

Check In:............................ Check Out:............................

Lodging:.................................. Park hours:.......................

Who I Went With:...

Fee(s):.. Will I Return? YES / NO

Rating ★ ★ ★ ★ ★

ABOUT THIS STATE PARK

Union County State Fish & Wildlife Area encompasses 6,202 acres in the Lower Mississippi River bottomlands division of Illinois. Numerous shallow sloughs and other water areas totaling approximately 1,100 acres are scattered throughout the area. More prominent water areas include Grassy Lake (350 acres) and Lyerla Lake (275 acres). Union County State Fish & Wildlife Area is a haven for many diverse forms of wildlife.

Activities

- ☐ ATV/OHV
- ☐ Berry Picking
- ☐ Biking
- ☐ Boating
- ☐ Canoeing
- ☐ Horseback Riding
- ☐ Kayaking
- ☐ Photography
- ☐ Skiing
- ☐ Skijoring
- ☐ Fishing
- ☐ Hiking
- ☐ Hunting
- ☐ Snowshoeing
- ☐ Swimming
- ☐ Wildlife
- ☐ Bird Viewing
- ☐ Snowmobiling
- ☐ ....
- ☐ ....

Facilities

- ☐ ADA
- ☐ Gift Shop
- ☐ Visitor Center
- ☐ Picnic Sites
- ☐ Museum
- ☐ Restrooms
- ☐ ....
- ☐ ....

Notes

....
....
....
....

Passport Stamps

VOLO BOG STATE NATURAL AREA

Lake

DATE(S) VISITED:...

☐ SPRING   ☐ SUMMER   ☐ FALL   ☐ WINTER

ABOUT THIS STATE PARK

Volo Bog State Natural Area is a nature reserve in Illinois, preserving Volo Bog. The bog was designated a National Natural Landmark in 1973 as the only remaining open-water quaking bog in Illinois. The site also contains woodlands, savanna, marshes, prairie restoration areas, shrubland and old fields. Volo Bog State Natural Area currently offers two major trails. An elevated 0.5-mile boardwalk leads from the Visitor Center into the bog itself. A 2.75-mile ground trail circles through the wetlands and meadows surrounding the bog.

WEATHER | **TEMP:**

☐ ☐ ☐ ☐ ☐ ☐

Check In:............................. Check Out:.............................

Lodging:................................ Park hours:.......................

Who I Went With:...

Fee(s):.. Will I Return?   YES / NO

Rating ★ ★ ★ ★ ★

Activities

☐ ATV/OHV   ☐ Horseback Riding   ☐ Fishing   ☐ Wildlife
☐ Berry Picking   ☐ Kayaking   ☐ Hiking   ☐ Bird Viewing
☐ Biking   ☐ Photography   ☐ Hunting   ☐ Snowmobiling
☐ Boating   ☐ Skiing   ☐ Snowshoeing   ☐ ....
☐ Canoeing   ☐ Skijoring   ☐ Swimming   ☐ ....

Facilities

☐ ADA   ☐ Visitor Center   ☐ Museum   ☐ ....
☐ Gift Shop   ☐ Picnic Sites   ☐ Restrooms   ☐ ....

Notes

....
....
....
....

Passport Stamps

WALNUT POINT STATE PARK

Douglas

DATE(S) VISITED:..

❑ SPRING   ❑ SUMMER   ❑ FALL   ❑ WINTER

WEATHER	TEMP:

☀   🌤   ☁   🌧   ⛈   🌨
❑   ❑   ❑   ❑   ❑   ❑

Check In:.............................. Check Out:................................

Lodging:................................. Park hours:........................

Who I Went With:...

Fee(s):... Will I Return?   YES / NO

Rating ★★★★★

ABOUT THIS STATE PARK

With its woods, water and wildlife, Walnut Point State Park in east-central Illinois has it all - from fishing, hunting and camping to hiking, picnicking and cross-country skiing. Conveniently located within a few miles of Interstate 57, U.S. Highway 36 and Illinois Route 133, the 671-acre site is 20 miles northeast of Charleston.

Activities

❑ ATV/OHV	❑ Horseback Riding	❑ Fishing	❑ Wildlife
❑ Berry Picking	❑ Kayaking	❑ Hiking	❑ Bird Viewing
❑ Biking	❑ Photography	❑ Hunting	❑ Snowmobiling
❑ Boating	❑ Skiing	❑ Snowshoeing	❑ ....
❑ Canoeing	❑ Skijoring	❑ Swimming	❑ ....

Facilities

❑ ADA	❑ Visitor Center	❑ Museum	❑ ....
❑ Gift Shop	❑ Picnic Sites	❑ Restrooms	❑ ....

Notes

....
....
....
....

Passport Stamps

WASHINGTON COUNTY STATE RECREATION AREA

Washington

DATE(S) VISITED:...

❏ SPRING ❏ SUMMER ❏ FALL ❏ WINTER

WEATHER	TEMP:
☀ ❄☁ ☁ ☔ ☔ ❄☁	
❏ ❏ ❏ ❏ ❏ ❏	

Check In:............................. Check Out:.............................

Lodging:................................. Park hours:........................

Who I Went With:..

Fee(s):.. Will I Return? YES / NO

Rating ★ ★ ★ ★ ★

ABOUT THIS STATE PARK

The beautiful Washington County Lake makes this site a special place for relaxing or fishing. Whether boating on its 248 acres, or fishing or hiking its 13-mile shoreline, the lake offers a perfect opportunity for family fun. This natural area has more than 900 acres for hunting, making it a paradise for shotgun or bow and arrow sportsmen. Whether camping, hunting, fishing, boating, hiking or picnicking.

Activities

❏ ATV/OHV
❏ Berry Picking
❏ Biking
❏ Boating
❏ Canoeing

❏ Horseback Riding
❏ Kayaking
❏ Photography
❏ Skiing
❏ Skijoring

❏ Fishing
❏ Hiking
❏ Hunting
❏ Snowshoeing
❏ Swimming

❏ Wildlife
❏ Bird Viewing
❏ Snowmobiling
❏ ....
❏ ....

Facilities

❏ ADA
❏ Gift Shop

❏ Visitor Center
❏ Picnic Sites

❏ Museum
❏ Restrooms

❏ ....
❏ ....

Notes

....
....
....
....

Passport Stamps

WAYNE FITZGERRELL STATE RECREATION AREA

Franklin, Jefferson

DATE(S) VISITED:..

❑ SPRING   ❑ SUMMER   ❑ FALL   ❑ WINTER

WEATHER	TEMP:
☀ ❑	🌤 ❑	☁ ❑	🌧 ❑	⛈ ❑	🌨 ❑

ABOUT THIS STATE PARK

Overlooking the U.S. Army Corps of Engineers' 19,000-acre Rend Lake Reservoir, Wayne Fitzgerrell SRA is a gateway to Southern Illinois' biggest outdoor playground - a paradise for outdoor recreation for all ages and interests. The park offers outstanding opportunities for hunting, fishing, camping, picnicking, horseback riding, hiking and other outdoor recreational pursuits.

Check In:............................ Check Out:...............................

Lodging:.................................... Park hours:........................

Who I Went With:..

Fee(s):.. Will I Return?   YES / NO

Rating ⭐ ⭐ ⭐ ⭐ ⭐

Activities

❑ ATV/OHV   ❑ Horseback Riding   ❑ Fishing   ❑ Wildlife
❑ Berry Picking   ❑ Kayaking   ❑ Hiking   ❑ Bird Viewing
❑ Biking   ❑ Photography   ❑ Hunting   ❑ Snowmobiling
❑ Boating   ❑ Skiing   ❑ Snowshoeing   ❑ ....
❑ Canoeing   ❑ Skijoring   ❑ Swimming   ❑ ....

Facilities

❑ ADA   ❑ Visitor Center   ❑ Museum   ❑ ....
❑ Gift Shop   ❑ Picnic Sites   ❑ Restrooms   ❑ ....

Notes

....
....
....
....

Passport Stamps

WEINBERG-KING STATE PARK

Schuyler

DATE(S) VISITED:...

❑ SPRING   ❑ SUMMER   ❑ FALL   ❑ WINTER

WEATHER						TEMP:
☀	☁	☁	☁	☁	☁	
❑	❑	❑	❑	❑	❑	

ABOUT THIS STATE PARK

Weinberg-King State Fish and Wildlife Area is an area of rolling hills with a meandering creek in western Illinois. The 772-acre site, including a 4-acre pond, is located in Schuyler County, 3 miles east of Augusta north of Route 101. Mrs. Gertrude K. Allen presented a deed for about 500 acres of what is now Weinberg-King SFWA land to the State of Illinois in May 1968. An additional 295 acres were later purchased by the Department of Natural Resources to expand the site.

Check In:............................. Check Out:.............................

Lodging:................................. Park hours:.......................

Who I Went With:...

Fee(s):... Will I Return?   YES / NO

Rating
⭐ ⭐ ⭐ ⭐ ⭐

Activities

❑ ATV/OHV	❑ Horseback Riding	❑ Fishing	❑ Wildlife
❑ Berry Picking	❑ Kayaking	❑ Hiking	❑ Bird Viewing
❑ Biking	❑ Photography	❑ Hunting	❑ Snowmobiling
❑ Boating	❑ Skiing	❑ Snowshoeing	❑ ....
❑ Canoeing	❑ Skijoring	❑ Swimming	❑ ....

Facilities

❑ ADA	❑ Visitor Center	❑ Museum	❑ ....
❑ Gift Shop	❑ Picnic Sites	❑ Restrooms	❑ ....

Notes
....
....
....
....

Passport Stamps

WELDON SPRINGS STATE RECREATION AREA | DeWitt

DATE(S) VISITED:..

☐ SPRING   ☐ SUMMER   ☐ FALL   ☐ WINTER

<table>
<tr><td colspan="2">WEATHER</td><td colspan="4">TEMP:</td></tr>
<tr><td>☀</td><td>❄</td><td>☁</td><td>🌧</td><td>🌦</td><td>🌨</td></tr>
<tr><td>☐</td><td>☐</td><td>☐</td><td>☐</td><td>☐</td><td>☐</td></tr>
</table>

ABOUT THIS STATE PARK

Located just southeast of Clinton in DeWitt County, Weldon Springs State Park is a 550-acre park for all seasons. Weldon Springs' recreational agenda is among the most comprehensive in the state park system, offering recreational opportunities year-round. During the milder seasons, you are invited to fish, boat, picnic, camp, hike, and view wildlife.

Check In:............................. Check Out:...............................

Lodging:.................................. Park hours:........................

Who I Went With:...

Fee(s):... Will I Return? YES / NO

Rating ★ ★ ★ ★ ★

Activities

☐ ATV/OHV   ☐ Horseback Riding   ☐ Fishing   ☐ Wildlife
☐ Berry Picking   ☐ Kayaking   ☐ Hiking   ☐ Bird Viewing
☐ Biking   ☐ Photography   ☐ Hunting   ☐ Snowmobiling
☐ Boating   ☐ Skiing   ☐ Snowshoeing   ☐ ....
☐ Canoeing   ☐ Skijoring   ☐ Swimming   ☐ ....

Facilities

☐ ADA   ☐ Visitor Center   ☐ Museum   ☐ ....
☐ Gift Shop ☐ Picnic Sites   ☐ Restrooms   ☐ ....

Notes

....
....
....
....

Passport Stamps

WHITE PINES FOREST STATE PARK

Ogle

DATE(S) VISITED:..

☐ SPRING   ☐ SUMMER   ☐ FALL   ☐ WINTER

WEATHER						TEMP:
☐	☐	☐	☐	☐	☐	

Check In:.............................. Check Out:..............................

Lodging:............................... Park hours:........................

Who I Went With:..

Fee(s):............................... Will I Return?   YES / NO

ABOUT THIS STATE PARK

Located in the heart of the Rock River valley, the 385-acre White Pines Forest State Park is the south boundary of the historic Chicago-Iowa Trail. Today, the park is perfect for family getaways to enjoy hiking, fishing, camping and picnicking. With serene, picturesque beauty, and modern lodge facilities amidst a beautiful forest, there is no better place to retreat from the everyday routine than the open spaces at White Pines.

Rating ★ ★ ★ ★ ★

Activities

☐ ATV/OHV	☐ Horseback Riding	☐ Fishing	☐ Wildlife
☐ Berry Picking	☐ Kayaking	☐ Hiking	☐ Bird Viewing
☐ Biking	☐ Photography	☐ Hunting	☐ Snowmobiling
☐ Boating	☐ Skiing	☐ Snowshoeing	☐ ....
☐ Canoeing	☐ Skijoring	☐ Swimming	☐ ....

Facilities

☐ ADA	☐ Visitor Center	☐ Museum	☐ ....
☐ Gift Shop	☐ Picnic Sites	☐ Restrooms	☐ ....

Notes

....
....
....
....

Passport Stamps

DATE(S) VISITED:...

❑ SPRING ❑ SUMMER ❑ FALL ❑ WINTER

WEATHER		TEMP:			
☀	❄☁	☁	🌧	🌧	🌨
❑	❑	❑	❑	❑	❑

ABOUT THIS STATE PARK

Named after Illinois Governor William G. Stratton, the park was developed in 1959 to provide boat access to the Illinois River. Any one of four public boat launching ramps will provide your start to an afternoon of boating, fishing or water-skiing. A jet ski launching area is located a short distance to the east of the boat ramps.

Check In:............................ Check Out:...............................

Lodging:................................. Park hours:........................

Who I Went With:..

Fee(s):... Will I Return? YES / NO

Rating ⭐⭐⭐⭐⭐

Activities

❑ ATV/OHV
❑ Berry Picking
❑ Biking
❑ Boating
❑ Canoeing

❑ Horseback Riding
❑ Kayaking
❑ Photography
❑ Skiing
❑ Skijoring

❑ Fishing
❑ Hiking
❑ Hunting
❑ Snowshoeing
❑ Swimming

❑ Wildlife
❑ Bird Viewing
❑ Snowmobiling
❑ ....
❑ ....

Facilities

❑ ADA
❑ Gift Shop

❑ Visitor Center
❑ Picnic Sites

❑ Museum
❑ Restrooms

❑ ....
❑ ....

Notes

....
....
....
....

Passport Stamps

WILLIAM W. POWERS STATE RECREATION AREA

Cook

DATE(S) VISITED:...

❑ SPRING   ❑ SUMMER   ❑ FALL   ❑ WINTER

ABOUT THIS STATE PARK

William W. Powers State Recreation Area, located on Wolf Lake on Chicago's far southeast side at the Illinois-Indiana state line, offers opportunities to get outdoors and enjoy nature in the city for residents and visitors. Wolf Lake provides outstanding fishing, about six miles of shoreline is available to bank fisherman. William W. Powers SRA is a great venue for nature education for area children and families, as well as for picnics and family outings.

WEATHER			TEMP:		
❑	❑	❑	❑	❑	❑

Check In:............................ Check Out:.............................

Lodging:................................... Park hours:.......................

Who I Went With:..

Fee(s):.. Will I Return?   YES / NO

Rating
★ ★ ★ ★ ★

Activities

❑ ATV/OHV   ❑ Horseback Riding   ❑ Fishing   ❑ Wildlife
❑ Berry Picking   ❑ Kayaking   ❑ Hiking   ❑ Bird Viewing
❑ Biking   ❑ Photography   ❑ Hunting   ❑ Snowmobiling
❑ Boating   ❑ Skiing   ❑ Snowshoeing   ❑ ....
❑ Canoeing   ❑ Skijoring   ❑ Swimming   ❑ ....

Facilities

❑ ADA   ❑ Visitor Center   ❑ Museum   ❑ ....
❑ Gift Shop   ❑ Picnic Sites   ❑ Restrooms   ❑ ....

Notes
....
....
....
....

Passport Stamps

WOLF CREEK STATE PARK

Shelby

DATE(S) VISITED:...

❏ SPRING ❏ SUMMER ❏ FALL ❏ WINTER

WEATHER				TEMP:	
☀	❄☁	☁	🌧	⛈	🌨
❏	❏	❏	❏	❏	❏

Check In:............................... Check Out:...............................

Lodging:................................... Park hours:........................

Who I Went With:..

Fee(s):.. Will I Return? YES / NO

Rating ⭐ ⭐ ⭐ ⭐ ⭐

ABOUT THIS STATE PARK

Eight miles northwest of Windsor, Wolf Creek State Park and the adjoining Eagle Creek State Recreation Area encompass 11,100 acres of water, 250 miles of shoreline and large tracts of carefully maintained indigenous woodlands ideal for camping, horseback riding, snowmobiling, boat fishing, water skiing, pontoon boating, windsurfing or just plain bobbing and drifting on the glittering expanse of the lake itself.

Activities

❏ ATV/OHV
❏ Berry Picking
❏ Biking
❏ Boating
❏ Canoeing

❏ Horseback Riding
❏ Kayaking
❏ Photography
❏ Skiing
❏ Skijoring

❏ Fishing
❏ Hiking
❏ Hunting
❏ Snowshoeing
❏ Swimming

❏ Wildlife
❏ Bird Viewing
❏ Snowmobiling
❏ ....
❏ ....

Facilities

❏ ADA
❏ Gift Shop

❏ Visitor Center
❏ Picnic Sites

❏ Museum
❏ Restrooms

❏ ....
❏ ....

Notes

....
....
....
....

Passport Stamps

DATE(S) VISITED:..

❑ SPRING   ❑ SUMMER   ❑ FALL   ❑ WINTER

WEATHER	TEMP:
☀ ❄☁ ☁ 🌧 🌧 🌨	
❑ ❑ ❑ ❑ ❑ ❑	

Check In:............................. Check Out:.............................

Lodging:.................................. Park hours:........................

Who I Went With:..

Fee(s):... Will I Return?   YES / NO

ABOUT THIS STATE PARK

Woodford State Fish and Wildlife Area is a picturesque area along the east side of the Illinois River. Among its features are many artesian wells, which make the manmade channels an excellent winter fishing area. The 2,900-acre site, of which 2,462-acres are water, is a favorite stopping point for waterfowl during migration.

Rating ⭐ ⭐ ⭐ ⭐ ⭐

Activities

❑ ATV/OHV	❑ Horseback Riding	❑ Fishing	❑ Wildlife
❑ Berry Picking	❑ Kayaking	❑ Hiking	❑ Bird Viewing
❑ Biking	❑ Photography	❑ Hunting	❑ Snowmobiling
❑ Boating	❑ Skiing	❑ Snowshoeing	❑ ....
❑ Canoeing	❑ Skijoring	❑ Swimming	❑ ....

Facilities

❑ ADA	❑ Visitor Center	❑ Museum	❑ ....
❑ Gift Shop	❑ Picnic Sites	❑ Restrooms	❑ ....

Notes

....
....
....
....

Passport Stamps

Made in the USA
Monee, IL
30 August 2024

64899222R00075